HISTORY OF INDIA

History of India

ISBN:978-81-8252-387-6

Published by:
Wilco
Publishing House
Mumbai, India

Tel: (91-22) 2204 1420 / 2284 2574
Fax: (91-22) 2204 1429
E mail:wilcos@vsnl.com

CONTENTS

Chapter - 1

The Indus Valley Civilization

Even five thousand years ago, the city was remarkably well-planned.

The earliest urban civilisation in India and in fact, one of the earliest civilisations in the world, was the Indus Valley Civilisation, or the Harappan Culture.

About 5000 years ago, a group of nomads travelled from Sumeria (present-day Iran) and entered North Western India, near present-day Karachi. By the banks of the River Indus, they found a land so richly fertile that they settled there without hesitation. This area, with abundant water, fodder and fuel, later came to be known as Punjab.

Over the next thousand years, the immigrants spread over an area of half a million square miles. Excavations prove that the level of urban planning and architecture prevalent here was incomparable. The anchor for this civilisation lay in the beautiful twin cities of Mohenjo-daro and Harappa.

Mohenjo-daro and Harappa were identical in most ways. Even centuries ago, they were remarkably well planned. Both cities were a square mile, with defensive outer walls. Each city block was built on a grid that was so perfectly proportioned that historians are baffled, even today.

The name Mohenjo-daro means 'Mound of the Dead' in Sindhi. The city was built around 2600 BC and abandoned around 1700 BC. Evidence indicates that the city was prone to devastating floods.

The street layout shows an understanding of the basic principles of traffic. The broad parallel streets ran in perfect patterns around the buildings, and crossed each other to divide the city into 12 rectangular blocks. The corners of the streets were rounded to allow the carts to turn easily. Except for the West-Central

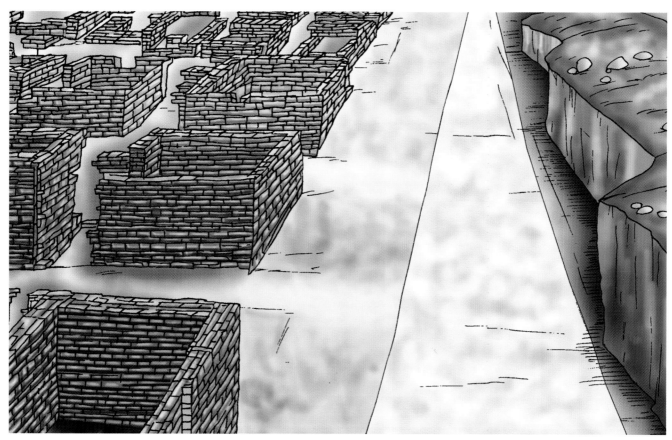

The streets of Mohenjo-daro.

Each house had a well from which it drew water.

blocks, the basic unit of city planning was the individual house.

The buildings were made of bricks – either baked mud or wood bricks. The baked bricks were a superior version of the sun-dried bricks used in other civilisations. Wooden bricks were made by burning wood.

The amazing part was that the workers made every brick of the same size! The type of bricks used, ensured the durability of the buildings. The flat roofs of the building were made from timber and in many houses, brick stairways led to the roofs.

Despite a population of about 30,000, the city had one of the best sanitation systems. Each house had a well from which it drew water.

From a bathing room the waste water was directed into covered drains along the main streets. Since all the streets were well-drained, the city remained dry and clean. This is evidence of a very modern method of sanitation and sewerage.

Advanced architecture showed in the construction of granaries, warehouses, platforms and protective walls.

Mohenjo-daro was primarily an agricultural city. It was situated below the great mountain ranges, with rivers flowing abundantly through the land, depositing rich soil. So it was obvious that agriculture was the main occupation.

Further proof of this is the presence of a large well, a central marketplace and several granaries in the city. One of the most important buildings was the Great Granary. This was designed in such a way as to enable easy unloading of carts that delivered grain from the countryside.

There were several granaries in the city.

The Great Bath

The Great Granary or the Great Hall had three major buildings. The earliest structure was represented by a single wall that was oriented East-West and lay directly below the second major building of the Great Hall. The Great Hall was first modified with the addition of an external mud-brick platform and subsequently completely filled with clay. On top of this new platform, the Later Hall was built. Once stored inside, the grain stayed fresh, thanks to the ducts that allowed air to circulate beneath and keep it dry.

Near the granary was the great public bath house, known as the Great Bath. Steps led down to a pool lined with bricks in a huge courtyard. The beautiful bath area had a layer of natural tar – this was to prevent it from leaking. In the centre of the bath area was the swimming pool. The purpose of the Great Bath was assumed to be for ritualistic bathing. This is a practice followed by Hindus even today.

Houses were well protected from noise, odour and thieves. Each house opened out onto inner courtyards and smaller lanes, so it was safe. Although some houses were larger than the others, the city seemed to promote an equal society, for all the houses had the same kind of access to water and drainage. So, it could be presumed that there was not much wealth concentration in the city.

The city had an impressive defense structure in place as well. Though it lacked outer walls, there were defensive towers in the West and South. Since other Indus cities had stronger defense systems in place, it is speculated that perhaps Mohenjo-daro was only an administrative center.

Houses were well protected from noise, odour and thieves.

Chapter - 2

The Decline of Harappan Culture

An Indus Valley Seal

The city itself was divided into two parts – the Citadel and the Lower City. The former contained the public bath and a large residential building that probaby housed around 5000 people. It also had two large assembly halls. There is no evidence that there were any Kings, priests or armies nor any palaces or temples. So the purpose of the Citadel is still unclear.

The Lower City was the one laid out in a grid pattern. Most of the city's inhabitants lived here and appeared to have been traders or artisans. They lived with others who were involved in the same occupation, in specific neighbourhoods. Shops with potters' kilns, dyers' vats, metal working, bead making, shell making – suggest a wide range of occupations. Materials were brought in from far-off lands to make a variety of things – seals, beads and other artifacts.

The seals that were excavated had pictures of animals, Gods and other inscriptions. Some of these were used to stamp clay on trade goods.

Objects from the Indus valley Civilisation have been found in Mesopotamia (present-day Iraq), present-day Afghanistan and in other parts of India.

The Indus Valley residents had access to gold and copper mining and the place was possibly a source of semi-precious stones. This can be seen in the jewellery discovered in the area.

The people of the city seemed to have good irrigation systems in place, as well as flood-control measures.

But despite this, evidence shows that Mohenjo-daro was destroyed and rebuilt seven times. This was mostly due to damage caused by terrible floods as the river changed its course around 3700 years ago and the city was wiped out. But the

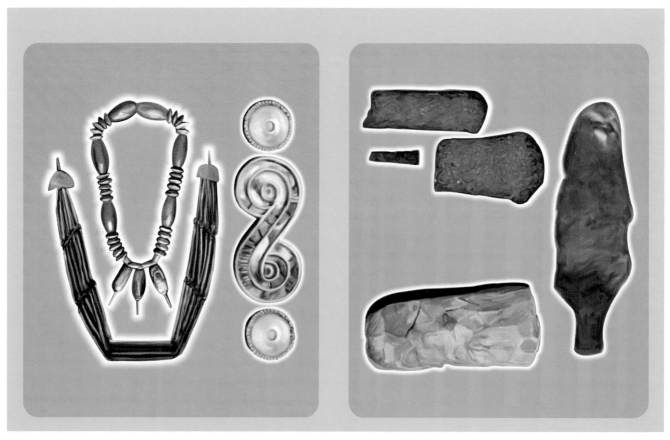

Jewellery discovered in the area.   *Tools used during this period.*

Dedicated architects dealt with nature's forces.

repeated rebuilding process proves that dedicated architects worked on it and dealt with nature's forces.

Harappan life was supported by extensive agricultural production and by commerce, which included trade with Sumer in Southern Mesopotamia (present-day Iraq).

The people made tools and weapons from copper and bronze but not iron. Cotton was woven and dyed for clothing; wheat, rice, and a variety of vegetables and fruits were cultivated; a number of animals, including the humped bull, were domesticated.

It appears that the Harappan people lived peaceful lives, with little fear of invasion. So, when the Aryan invaders arrived from the Northwest, they hardly encountered any resistance. They overpowered the Harappans with superior military skills.

The Dancing Girl   *The sculpture of a Priest King.*

One by one, all the cities fell, already much weakened by constant floods and rebuilding. The cities were emptied of population. The Harappans, who were termed 'Dasyus' by the Aryans, either joined the lowest level in Aryan society or fled South.

The fall of Mohenjo-daro is a typical example of the decay of this great culture. It took another thousand years before a city as well-planned as this was built again.

Later excavations revealed a technologically advanced culture and an efficient system of governance as well.

Some of the surviving artifacts from that era include soapstone seals like the humped Brahmani bull and Pashupati. Other carved figurines that survived are the bronze dancing girl, the statue of a priest and a man's torso.

Stone implements and cave paintings from this period have been discovered in many parts of South Asia. Evidence of domestication of animals, permanent village

Wheel-turned pottery

settlements, and wheel-turned pottery dating from the middle of the sixth Century B.C. has been found in the foothills of Sindh and Baluchistan, both in present-day Pakistan.

Archeologists like R. D. Bannerjee and Sir John Marshall rediscovered this historic site in the 1920's and gave the world a peek into ancient culture and civilisation.

Chapter - 3

ANCIENT INDIA
The Vedic Age

The Aryan invaders lived in circular huts.

The Aryan invaders were primarily nomads. They were not accustomed to the urban way of life. Thus, they did not occupy the beautiful cities they had conquered. Instead, they cleared forests near the riverbanks and settled in small villages, or Gramas, becoming semi-agriculturists. Perhaps, their fear of permanent dwellings prevented them from moving into the cities. Each Grama was headed by a Gramani.

The Aryan villages were simple structures, which formed the basis for architecture in India for thousands of years. In fact, the caves of Ajanta and Ellora were influenced by early Aryan villages. Their huts were very basic, circular and

The priests, the commandants and the administration assisted the King.

with thatched roofs over bamboo logs. People, who were better off, used planks of wood or tiles as roofs and unbaked bricks for walls. Later, the huts became rectangular with barrel-shaped roofs. Fences of wood and bamboo surrounded the settlement for protection against wild animals.

Soon, the demand for fertile land grew and rivalry spread. Groups of villages joined forces and thus small 'cities' or clans called 'Vis' were born. A group or clan formed a Jana and their leader was the Rajan or King. A priest or Purohita, the commandant or Senani, and the administration, Sabha and Samiti, assisted him.

The city buildings were made almost entirely from wood, and walls protected each city. The Vedic carpenters became skilled at constructing timber structures and their techniques were used in stone constructions of the future.

The Vedic cities were divided into four quadrants with two main roads intersecting at the center. Each quadrant housed a citadel, the residential area, the merchants and traders. Animal husbandry, agriculture, weaving, carpentry and metalworking were the primary occupations. The barter system flourished. External trade began with West Asia and Egypt. Coins were introduced for trade and were called Nishka.

The Aryans relied on nature and worshipped its various aspects – the animals, the wind, the trees, the sky, water and other things. Prayers were offered to Agni, Vayu and Surya. Common rituals included Yagas and Yajnas (sacred fires and sacrifices). Rituals like Rajasuya or royal consecration, Vajapeya or chariot race and Ashvamedha or horse sacrifice were widespread.

The Aryans made the single largest contribution to Indian religion through the language of Sanskrit. It was during this age that the Vedas were composed. And this formed the foundation for the early Hindu religion.

The Aryans developed a rich tradition, composing hymns of the four Vedas. These

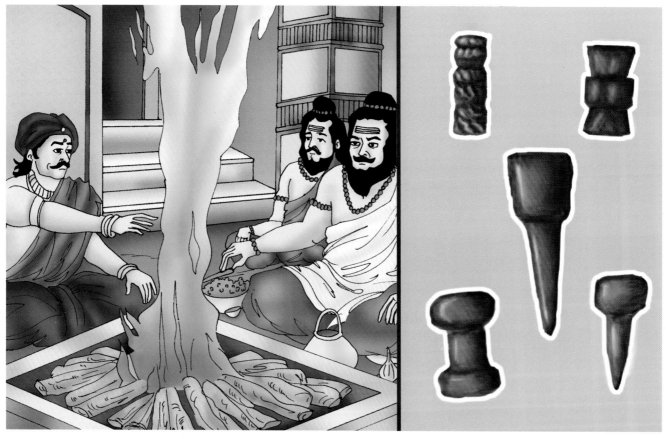

Prayers were offered to Agni, Vayu and Surya.   *Nishka Coins*

| A scene from 'The Mahabharata' | A scene from 'The Ramayana' |

sacred scriptures included the: Rig Veda, Sama Veda, Yajur Veda and Atharva Veda.

Two of the greatest epics were also composed during this period, 'The Ramayana' and 'The Mahabharata'. These tell us a great deal about the culture, society and religion of the people of that era.

Religious practices were very stringent in the Vedic age and were governed by a series of rituals. With a staunch belief in God, every aspect of life was complicated through endless rituals. Animals were sacrificed on a daily basis to appease the Gods. No one dared to speak against the priests or Brahmins. Soon, this class became very powerful as no one else could perform the complex rituals.

It was during the Vedic Age that the Caste System was born. Due to work specialisation, different classes of society developed. Besides the Brahmins, there

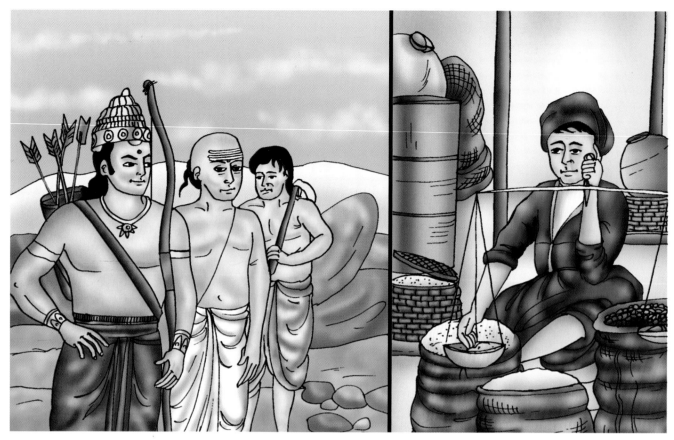

A Kshatriya, a Brahmin and a Shudra.   A Vaishya

were the Kshatriyas or warriors, the Vaishyas or merchants and Shudras or the outcasts, who performed menial jobs like scavenging, fishing and removing dead bodies.

With time, the powers of the King grew. By 500 BC, sixteen monarchies and republics known as the Mahajanapadas - Kasi, Kosala, Anga, Magadha, Vajji (or Vriji), Malla, Chedi, Vatsa (or Vamsa), Kuru, Panchala, Machcha (or Matsya), Surasena, Assaka, Avanti, Gandhara, Kamboja stretched across the Indo-Gangetic plains from present-day Afghanistan, the Punjab (in Pakistan and also in India), and the fringes of Western Uttar Pradesh.

The status of the Brahmins and Kshatriyas improved greatly and the common people had little or no say in the administration. A lot of importance was placed on pronouncing the Vedic verses correctly, as it was believed, that this led to prosperity and success in war. Kshatriyas became richer and used the services of Brahmins. The other castes were degraded and reached the lower rungs of society.

Chapter - 4

A Time for Reform - Buddha

An astrologer predicted that Siddhartha was destined to live the life of a sage.

At such a time, when class distinctions were high and rituals formed the very foundation of every single aspect of daily life, there came two reformers who changed the way of thinking, Gautam Buddha and Mahavira.

Buddha was born as Prince Siddhartha, son of the King and Queen of Kapilavastu, Shuddhodana and Mayadevi around 566 BC. The Kingdom was located on the borders of present-day Nepal. Siddhartha or Gautama, as he was also known, was born into the Kshatriya caste of the Shakya clan.

Soon after his birth, an astrologer predicted that the boy was destined to live the life of a sage. He would eventually give up his right to the throne and all worldly pleasures. The parents of the boy were shattered. They decided to prevent him from being exposed to life outside the palace and kept a close watch on him.

Siddhartha saw an old man, weak and frail.

Thus, young Siddhartha never left the palace and saw nothing more than the luxuries of the palace. His parents hoped that he would get so used to such a rich lifestyle that he would never give it up.

When he was 16, his father got him married to Yashodhara, the beautiful daughter of a nobleman. The King was gleeful that his son now had one more worldy attachment that he would not shirk.

The older Siddhartha grew, the more curious he became. One day he summoned his charioteer and demanded that he be taken on a tour of the city. The first person they came across was an old man, weak and frail, by the side of the road. Siddhartha was intrigued by him, and was told that with old age comes weakness and ill health.

The next person they came across was a sick man in great pain. Siddhartha learned that the man was not immune from diseases. Then, they saw a dead body being carried to the cremation ground. The young Prince was told that everyone would die one day and leave the world.

Finally, Siddhartha saw a sage, serene and calm. He heard that such holy men renounced their worldly possessions and desires.

Siddhartha was deeply troubled by his first experience of the outside world. Questions about life and death plagued him constantly. As the days passed, he became more and more miserable. One day, he decided that to learn the answers to his questions, he would have to leave his luxurious life.

He left the palace that night, while his wife and son slept. He was only 29 years old.

Siddhartha wandered far, trying different ways to find the path to Truth. Finally, he reached the city of Bodhgaya and started to meditate under a large fig tree near

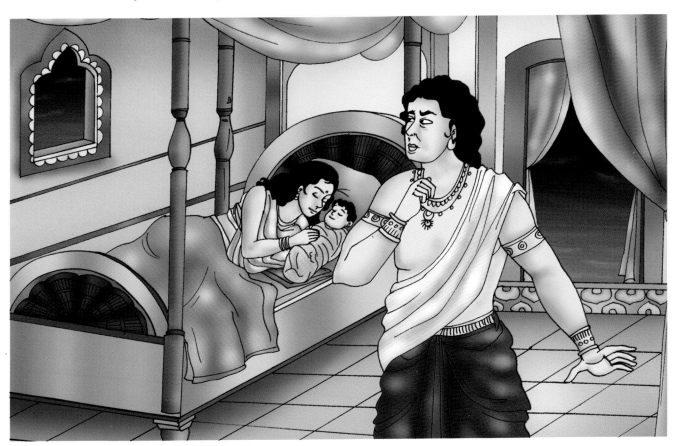

Siddhartha left the palace that night while his wife and son slept.

Buddha under the Bodhi tree.

the Mahabodhi temple, determined not to rise until fully enlightened.

After 49 days of meditation, at the age of 35, he attained Enlightenment. Gautama, from then on, was known as the Buddha or "Awakened One." Buddha is also sometimes translated as "The Enlightened One." He was named after the Bodhi tree under which he meditated.

It is said that the tree has been destroyed time and again, by man and nature, but it continues to spring up again, without fail. The tree is worshipped as a sign of Buddha's presence.

The Enlightened One shared his knowledge with five sanyasis who meditated near him. His first sermon on 'The Turning Wheel of Dharma' was held at the Deer Garden. After that, he travelled all over the country, sharing the knowledge with the common people in the simplest language so that they would understand.

He started to travel around teaching the key principles of Buddhism. These were called Noble Truths:

- The world is full of suffering and misery

- Desire is the main reason for this suffering and misery

- Suffering and misery can be removed by removing desire

- Desire can be overcome by following the Eight-Fold Path

The Eight-Fold Path included: Right Views, Right Thoughts, Right speech, Right Actions, Right Livelihood, Right Efforts, Right Mindfulness and Right Meditation.

Buddha taught that every man controlled his own fate or destiny and it was not in the hands of God. He criticized Vedic customs and rituals and demanded to know why Brahmins were considered superior.

Buddha teaches the Eight-Fold path.

25

Buddha travelled dressed in his saffron robes and taking along his begging bowl.

Buddha preached non-violence, peace and harmony. He believed that people should treat each other with compassion, forgiveness and tolerance. He encouraged his followers to lead a balanced life, one that was neither severe nor luxurious.

He had a large number of followers, especially in Magadha, Kosala and the neighbouring areas. Whenever he travelled, he would be dressed in his saffron robes and would take along only his begging bowl and stick.

Buddha now established a community of monks called 'Sangha'. With them, he travelled far and wide, spreading his teachings and performing many miracles. In Shravasti, there is a story that tells how, on his throwing down the seed of a mango, a great mango tree instantly arose. Another story tells how the Buddha stood in the air, the lower part of his body engulfed in flames, with five hundred jets of water streaming from the top of his body.

The Kanheri Cave Temple

Buddhism has now spread not only in India but abroad as well. Burma, China, Japan and several other South Eastern countries follow this religion ardently.

Several monuments in India are tributes to Buddhism. These include temples and universities at Sanchi, Bharhut, Amaravati, Nagarjunakonda and others. The famous Buddhist Cave Temples – Ajanta, Ellora, Kanheri and Karla are in Maharashtra in Western India.

In 483 BC, the beloved monk passed away. Though he lived centuries ago, his birthday is still celebrated as Buddha Jayanti in India. The Bodhi Tree is still worshipped as the symbol of Enlightenment.

Mahavira, too, was the son of a King, and was a very spiritual boy even during his childhood. Constantly meditating, he was a compassionate young man with no desire to take over the Kingdom. Finally, renouncing his rights to the throne, he

Statue of Mahavira   *Jains*

travelled around as an ascetic, teaching the path to spiritual freedom. His devotees were divided into four groups Sadhu (monks), Sadhvi (nuns), Shravak (laymen) and Shravika (laywomen). Later, they came to be known as Jains.

He taught them the four vows of Parshva and the principle of chastity. He asked everyone to embrace the principles of non-violence, truthfulness, non-stealing and non-possession.

His teachings greatly impressed the masses and he soon became a religious icon, the founder of a new religion called Jainism.

Both reformers undermined the role of the priest as the mediator between the people and God. The new religions were roughly based on the Hindu doctrines. Long after the two reformers left the world, their teachings continue to be followed.

Chapter - 5

Persian and Greek Invaders

Persian King Darius   *Alexander the Great*

In 520 BC the Persian Kings, Darius and Cyrus invaded Northwest India and conquered the Indus Valley. The Persians ruled that part of India for about a century and a half.

In the meantime, Aryan Kingdoms continued to flourish in the East.

Soon after, the Greeks, headed by Alexander the Great of Macedonia, invaded parts of Northwestern India. Conquering lands along the way, Alexander's army crossed the Indus and engaged in an epic battle with the local ruler of Punjab, Raja Puru or King Porus. After Alexander's victory, he was so impressed with Puru's bravery that he made an alliance with him and appointed him General of the land.

Although Alexander won, his troops rebelled and refused to go any further than

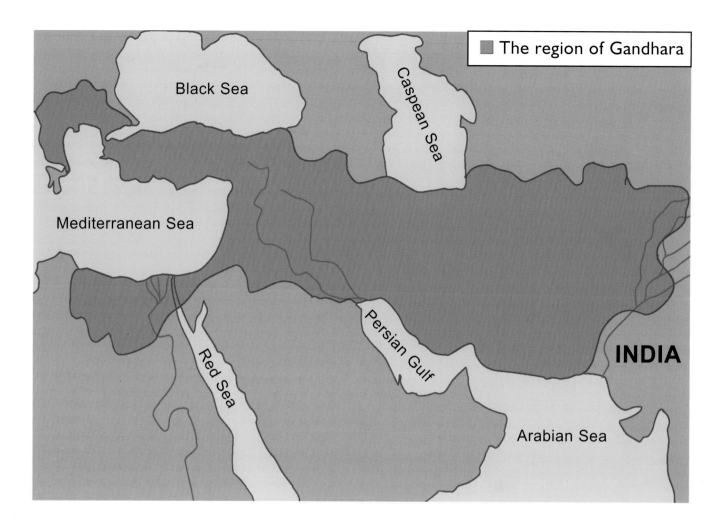

present-day Jalandhar. They had heard rumours that a mighty Indian army waited on the other side to fight them. The Indus river, thus marks the end of his conquered lands. Soon Alexander left India, after naming some of his generals as governors or satraps of the conquered provinces. But in a few years, Indian forces chased out most of the generals.

Both Persian and Greek invasions greatly influenced the political systems of India. The region of Gandhara (today's Afghanistan and Northwestern Pakistan) became a mix of cultures – Indian, Persian, Central Asian and Greek. This gave rise to a new culture, Greco-Buddhism. This lasted till the 5th Century.

Chapter - 6

The Maurya Dynasty

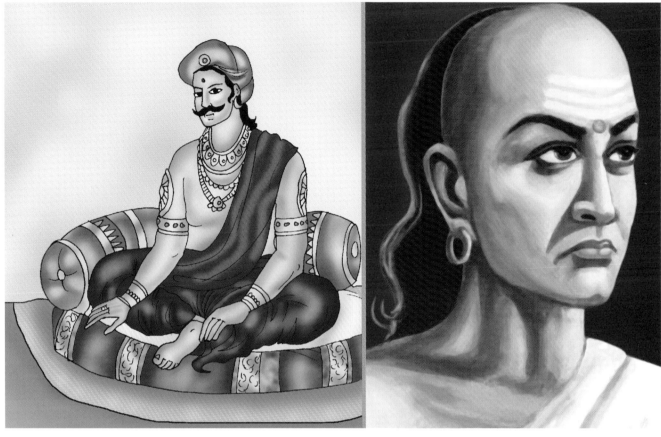

King Chandragupta   Chanakya

After Alexander's departure, a powerful ruler named Chandragupta Maurya invaded Central and Western India. By 316 BC the empire, with its capital at Pataliputra (near modern-day Patna), had fully occupied Northwestern India.

The King was aided in his conquests by his famous minister, Chanakya (also known as Kautilya). In fact, it was Chanakya who encouraged Chandragupta to take over Magadha from the Nanda dynasty. Chandragupta used an intelligence network, gathering many young men from across Magadha and other provinces. These were the men upset over the corrupt rule of King Dhana of Magadha. Chandragupta then gathered enough resources needed for his army to fight a long series of battles. These men included the former General of Taxila, other accomplished students of Chanakya, the representative of the Himalayan King

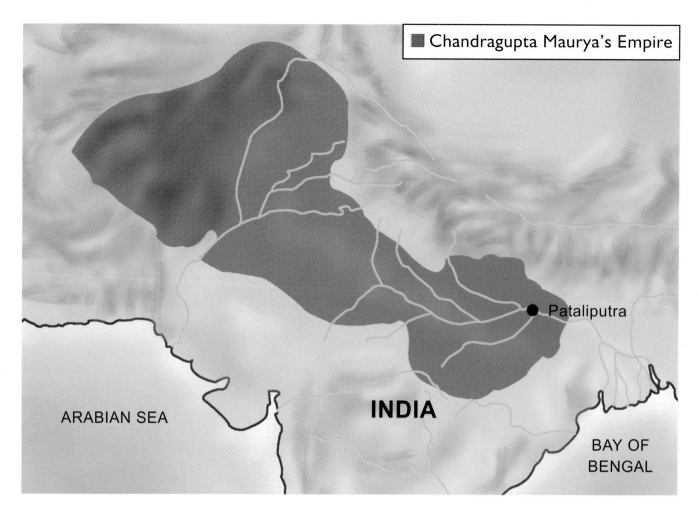

Porus of Kakayee, his son Malayketu, and the rulers of small states.

Slowly, and with an elaborate plan in place, Chandragupta Maurya took over the throne of Magadha.

The Empire went on to become one of the most widespread and powerful political and military rule in India. The Empire stretched to the North along the boundaries of the Himalayas and to the East (today's Assam). To the West, it reached present-day Pakistan and large parts of Afghanistan.

Under Chandragupta and his successors, trade and agriculture flourished, thanks to a single, efficient system of finance and administration.

Chanakya, in the meantime, went on to write the 'Arthashastra', one of the greatest collection of essays on economics, politics, foreign affairs, administration, military arts, war and religion, ever produced.

Seleucus I and Chandragupta signed a peace treaty.

Chandragupta established a single currency across India. He put in place a network of regional governors and administrators. A sound civil service provided justice and security for merchants, farmers and traders. The Mauryan army wiped out gangs of bandits, private armies and powerful chiefs who tried to establish their supremacy. The Mauryans also sponsored many public works and waterways to enhance productivity.

In 305 BC, Chandragupta was once again in conflict with the Greeks. Seleucus I, ruler of the Seleucid Empire, launched a campaign to reconquer parts of Northwest India. The campaign failed and the two rulers signed a peace treaty. The Greek ruler received from Chandragupta, 500 war elephants that played an important role in his future conquests abroad.

The Greeks and the Indians then maintained good relations with each other. Several Greek historians and scholars like Megasthenes, Deimakos and Dionysius

Chandragupta renounced the throne and joined a group of Jain monks.

attended Chandragupta's court.

Under Chandragupta Maurya, the religious movement of Jainism gained popularity. Thousands of Jain temples and stupas were built during the reign of the Mauryas. As Chandragupta grew old, he renounced the throne and joined a group of wandering Jain monks.

Chandragupta was succeeded by his son, Bindusara, around 298 BC. After him came one of the greatest emperors India has ever had, Ashokavardhan Maurya, better known as Ashoka the Great.

Chapter - 7

Ashoka the Great

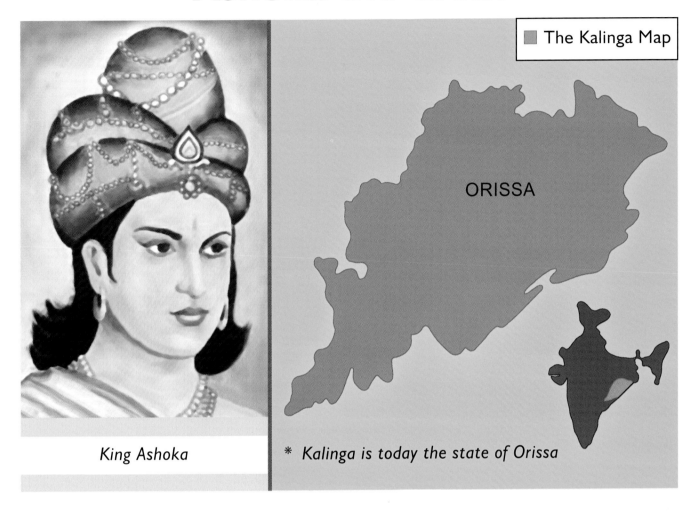

King Ashoka

The Kalinga Map

ORISSA

Kalinga is today the state of Orissa

As a young King, Ashoka was a mighty warrior, ambitious and greedy. He asserted the Empire's hold in Southern and Western India. He waged several wars and conquered lands far and wide.

But, one event, the Kalinga war, changed the entire course of his life. Kalinga was a rich and fertile land situated between the Godavari and Mahanadi rivers. That was the only land that was untouched by the Mauryan rule. Kalinga forms what is today the State of Orissa.

The people of Kalinga were fiercely independent and had refused to bow down to Ashoka's rule for years. One day, Ashoka heard the rumour that they were going to attack his Kingdom. Furious, he gathered his armies and marched to Kalinga.

Ashoka was filled with remorse.

A fierce battle ensued. Swords glinted dangerously, drawing blood, and wails of pain; arrows flew back and forth taking lives. The Kalinga army was fearless and was not ready to give up.

Brave though they were, the Kalinga soldiers were no match for Ashoka's power and skill. Soon, the Kalinga army was defeated and Ashoka won the most glorious victory of his life.

But strangely, he felt no joy. He stood on the battlefield looking out at the hundreds of bodies that lay there. He was filled with remorse, realising that the war had been pointless and had just succeeded in creating widows and orphans.

Ashoka then wept in grief and regret. The terrible sights he had seen haunted his dreams and every waking moment. He finally made a momentous decision: to stop fighting any more wars.

Ashoka gave up hunting and forbade the killing of animals except for food.

Ashoka now turned to Dharma or righteousness. He found solace in the teachings of Buddha. He embraced the message of love and kindness that Buddhism taught.

He now made a number of changes in his empire. He gave up hunting and forbade the killing of animals except for food. He ruled that all religions were equal and that none was superior to the other.

He began a campaign to spread Dharma across the country. He traveled widely, ordering the laws of Dharma to be etched on stone pillars and rocks to ensure that they would remain forever and be readily available for people to read and practice.

To this day, his carvings are found in Madhya Pradesh, Gujarat, Uttar Pradesh, Maharashtra, Orissa, Andhra Pradesh and Karnataka. Outside the country, these inscriptions have been found in Peshawar, Pakistan and Kandahar in Afghanistan. They have also been found on the borders of Nepal.

Ashoka erected several pillars, stupas and Buddhist viharas (dormitories) all over India. The stupas of Sanchi are world famous, especially the stupa named Sanchi Stupa I. The Ashoka Pillar at Sarnath is the most popular of the relics left by Ashoka. A fifty-foot tall stone pillar stands proudly at the top of which are carved four majestic lions. Today, the Ashoka pillar as it is known, is the official emblem of the Government of India. The Ashoka Chakra, found at the bottom of the pillar, now adorns the flag of India. This symbol stands for kingship and earthly rule. The Government's adoption of this symbol is indeed a true tribute to the great King.

Ashoka also paid great attention to education. He founded the University of Magadha in Nalanda and its students were learned and much respected.

Ashoka Pillar   Sanchi Stupa I

Chapter - 8

Prosperity under Ashoka's rule

The Empire blossomed under Ashoka's rule.

Ashoka developed his Kingdom by building canals for agriculture; roads to encourage business and trade, guesthouses for travellers and provided free medical aid for the common man.

The Empire blossomed under his rule. Beautiful trees lined wide roads, many of which were rare fruit trees and medicinal plants brought from far-off places. He was the first Emperor to build a hospital for the treatment of animals.

Ashoka lived for his people, working hard without any rest, teaching them the right way to live their lives. There was happiness and peace in the Kingdom. Neighbouring Kingdoms, which he could easily have conquered, became reliable allies.

Ashoka's children, Mahendra, Sanghamitra, Kunala, Teevala and Thishya also converted to Buddhism and travelled around spreading their father's ideas.

But all was not rosy in the Kingdom for long. For seventeen years everything had run smoothly. But after that, some of the Buddhist monks began to misbehave, became lazy and gave in to evil ways. Ashoka received reports from his trusted officers.

Ashoka then invited all serious-minded monks to a conference at Pataliputra. Soon, a large number of monks from all over the country gathered at Ashokarama in Pataliputra and a religious conference began. Ashoka's son Thishya presided over the conference. Ashoka spoke to each and every monk. He asked them many questions and discussed Buddhist teachings and principles.

Ashoka spoke to each and every monk.

Ashoka built cave dwellings.

After the conference, Buddhism gained new strength. Ashoka now spread the religion to far-off places by sending Buddhist monks. Soon, there were monks in Syria, Egypt, Macedonia, Burma and Kashmir, teaching the virtues of the religion. His own children, Mahendra and Sanghamitra, were sent to Ceylon (Sri Lanka) to spread Buddhism. In fact, it is due to Ashoka's efforts that Buddhism spread to all the countries of East Asia.

Ashoka also built cave dwellings, rest houses and Buddha viharas (dormitories) in large numbers, which testify not only to his dedication but also his penchant for skillful architecture. All his messages were written in Prakrit rather then the Sanskrit language. While translating these scripts, historians have learned the bulk of what is known of the Mauryan Empire.

By now Ashoka's Empire had spread and included a large part of India, Afghanistan, Baluchistan, Nepal, Bengal, Bihar, Andhra Pradesh and a big portion of today's Karnataka. Several of his inscriptions have been found in these places.

Ashoka now reorganized his Empire. He divided the Empire into four provinces Malava, Punjab, Dakshinapatha and Kalinga. Takshashila, Ujjain, Suvarnagiri and Kosala were the capitals.

Thus, prosperity continued till Ashoka grew old. Sadly, his old age was not one of peace and serenity. Since his sons were busy travelling the world and spreading his teachings, a quarrel arose over who would succeed Ashoka. His grandsons, Dasharatha and Samprati, were each anxious to be the next emperor.

In the last years of his life, Ashoka became frustrated with the petty fighting and

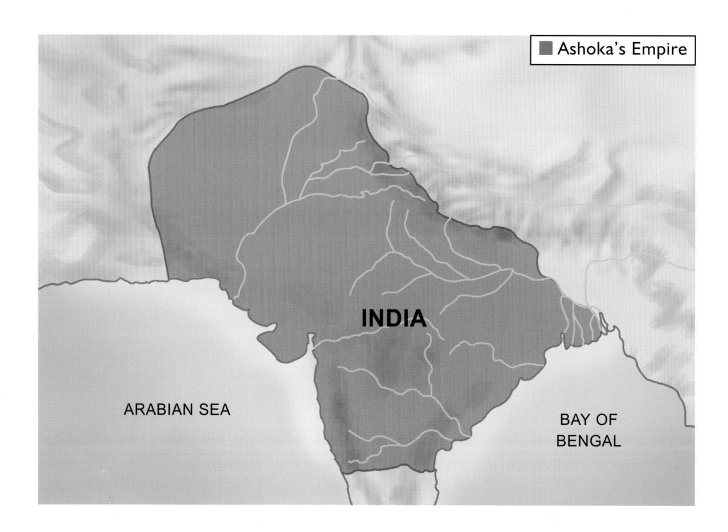

Ashoka lived like a monk.

took off on a pilgrimage. After wandering around, he finally reached Takshashila and stayed there.

He lived as a monk – fasting, meditating and leading an austere life. He also focused all his energy on the teachings of Buddhism.

At the age of 72, in 232 BC, Ashoka breathed his last. He left behind a reputation as an able ruler, a righteous lawmaker, a hero, a monk and a noble preacher of Dharma. That is why another name for him is Devanampriya Priyadarshi. The first name means 'beloved of the Gods' and the second "One whose appearance brings joy'.

Though it has been more than 2000 years since his death, his legacy of truth, love and compassion lives on in the minds of people across the world.

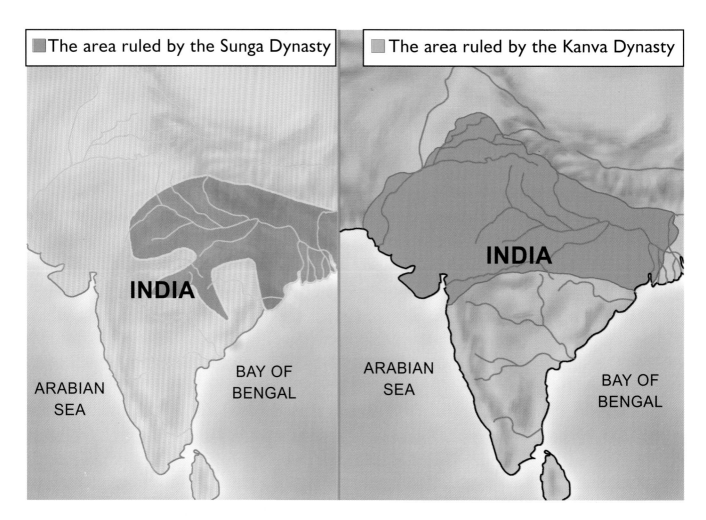

The area ruled by the Sunga Dynasty

The area ruled by the Kanva Dynasty

INDIA

ARABIAN SEA

BAY OF BENGAL

INDIA

ARABIAN SEA

BAY OF BENGAL

Ashoka was the last of the great Kings of the Mauryan dynasty. Those who succeeded him were not as capable or dynamic and could not continue the Maurya dynasty for long.

In 184 BC, the last of the Mauryan Kings was killed and the Sunga dynasty was established. This was followed by the Kanva dynasty but these did not last long.

Chapter - 9

The Guptas

Chandragupta - I   Samudragupta

After the decline of the Mauryans, the most significant rule was established by the Gupta Dynasty.

First came Chandragupta I, who revived the Empire in the North. He first conquered Magadha and set up his capital there. From there, he brought together a large part of Northeastern India. The ruler also revived many of Ashoka's doctrines of running the government.

After Chandragupta I came his son Samudra Gupta. He was a great warrior, a mighty ruler and a patron of arts. He started to expand the Kingdom and would not rest until he had conquered almost the whole of India.

First, he attacked the neighbouring Kingdoms; then he moved on to Bengal, Nepal and Assam. Towards the South, along the Bay of Bengal, he defeated many Kingdoms. In the West he extended his Kingdom in Khandesh and Palaghat.

Almost single-handedly, he unified most of India under one political power. He now took on the title of 'Maharajadhiraja' meaning 'The King of Kings'.

He also created a new monetary system. He minted different types of solid gold coins - Standard, Archer, Battle Axe, Ashvamedha, King and Queen, Tiger Slayer and Lyrist. The coins were beautifully sculpted and are proof of the fine quality of artisans of that era.

Samudra Gupta had a keen interest in music and his court was always filled with poets and scholars. He paid a lot of attention to religion, literature and culture. He

Samudra Gupta minted different types of solid gold coins.

Chandragupta II or Vikramaditya

Silver coins

himself was an accomplished veena player.

After Samudra Gupta came his son, Chandragupta II or Vikramaditya. He was one of the most powerful rulers of the Gupta Empire. Under him, the Empire expanded and reached the pinnacle of success.

His greatest victory was the one over the Shaka-Kshatrapa dynasty and the annexing of their Kingdom in Gujarat.

Chandragupta II controlled a vast empire, from the mouth of the Ganges to that of the Indus River and from what is now North Pakistan down to the Narmada. Pataliputra continued to be the capital of his huge Empire but Ujjain too, became almost like a second capital. Chandragupta II also minted silver coins in the Shaka tradition.

Chapter - 10

The Golden Age of the Guptas

Wall painting of Ajanta Cave.

Iron pillar - Delhi

The era of the Gupta Dynasty came to be known as the Golden Age of Indian culture. This period produced magnificent architecture, sculpture and painting. Proof of these are the marvellous wall paintings of the Ajanta Caves near Aurangabad in Maharashtra. They are considered to be among the greatest works of art in Indian culture. The Ajanta Caves are a cluster of 48 caves, carved out of rock and filled with Buddhist sculptures. The paintings depict the various lives of Buddha. It also provides an account of the daily life in India during that period.

The stone temples at Deogarh in Jhansi and at Bhitergaon in Kanpur prove the existence of brilliant architects at the time. Another area that amazes present-day historians is the metal work done during the Gupta period. Beautiful copper statues of Buddha found in many places, the Iron Pillar at Delhi and other amazing art forms give proof of the exquisite metal craftsmanship.

Another rock temple at Elephanta Island near Mumbai was also established in this period. A huge 18-foot statue of a three-headed Shiva stands proud and tall at this place. The three heads represent the Creator, Preserver and Destroyer. The Golden Age also saw the construction of several Hindu temples.

Poetry flourished during this period, producing one of the greatest poets of all time, Kalidasa. The peotry of the Gupta period was usually religious and meditative, lyrical, narrative or drama. Kalidasa excelled at lyrical poetry, but it is for his dramas that he is best remembered (like 'Shakuntala' and 'Meghdoot').

Significant achievements were made in music, education, mathematics, art, sculpture, Sanskrit literature and drama. Gupta literature consists of fables and folktales written in Sanskrit. These stories spread West to Persia, Egypt, and Greece, and became the basis for many Islamic literary works such as 'Ali Baba and

18-foot statue of three-headed Shiva; rock temple at Elephanta.

the Forty Thieves' and 'Aladdin and his Magic Lamp'.

Religious practices followed during this period formed the basis for modern Hinduism. Some of them were the worship of different deities, idol worship and construction and visits to temples.

Buddhism had opened up communication with foreigners and Chinese missionaries often visited India to pay their respects at the sacred places.

There were major advancements in science and mathematics in the Gupta period. The numeral system was an Indian invention, sometimes mistakenly attributed to the Arabs. They merely took it from India to Europe where it replaced the Roman system. The decimal system too, is an invention of this period. Aryabhatta's astronomy theories gave calculations of the Solar Year and

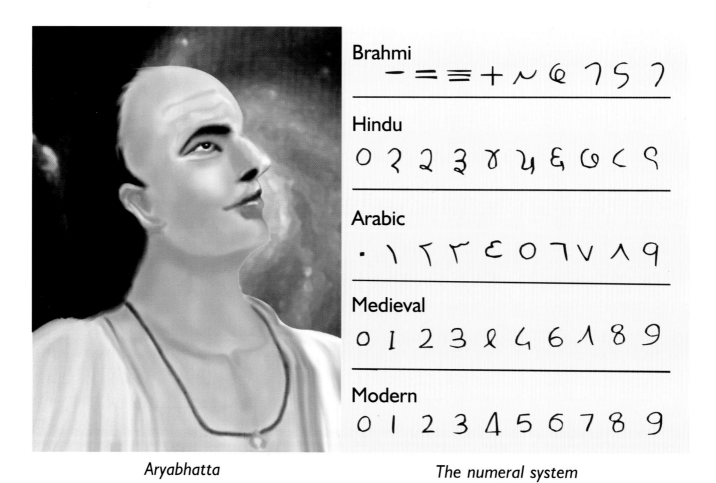

Aryabhatta

The numeral system

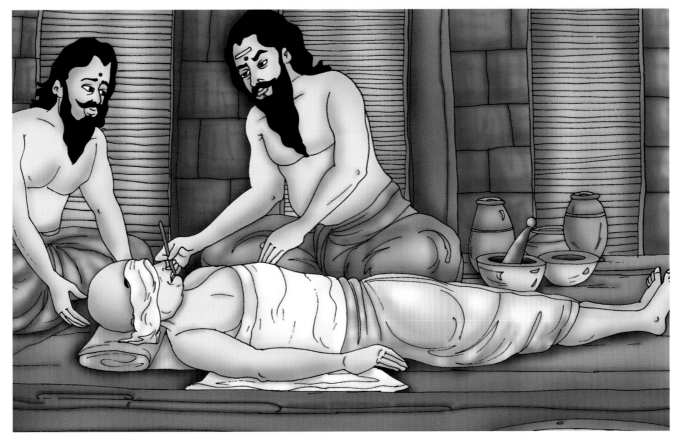

Physicians developed herbal remedies and a primitive form of plastic surgery.

the shape and movement of astral bodies with amazing accuracy.

Physicians developed herbal remedies and treated several illnesses. In fact, even a primitive form of plastic surgery was developed for the treatment of injuries to the face. Progress in physiology and biology was hindered because religion prohibited any contact with dead bodies. Dissection and anatomy studies were discouraged. Nevertheless, Indian physicians excelled in minor surgeries, caesarean section, bone-setting and skin grafting.

There was economic prosperity and peace in the country. The Guptas established a strong central government and at the same time, allowed a lot of local control. Kings were allowed to remain as vassal Kings. The Guptas did not believe in consolidating every Kingdom into a single administrative unit.

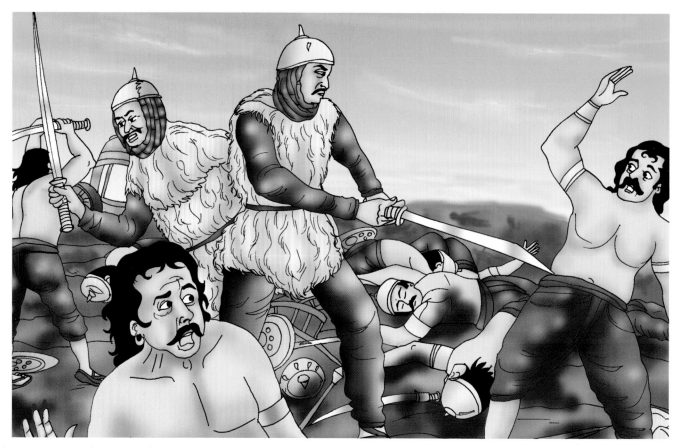

A race of people called the Huns started to attack the Gupta Empire.

However, the period of the Guptas soon came to an end. There was a race of people called the Huns from Central Asia, who migrated to India and started to attack the Gupta Empire. Soon, they had taken over Northern and Western India. The last of the Guptas perished. But many of their cultural and intellectual achievements were saved and passed on to other cultures and live on today.

Chapter - 11

Harsha Vardhana

Harsha was crowned as the King.

After the downfall of the Gupta Empire, in the middle of the sixth Century, Northern India broke up into small republics and monarchy states. The Huns had taken over Punjab and parts of Central India. But over the years, they became a part of the native population and their power weakened.

The ruler of Sthanvisvara, Thanesar in present-day Haryana, Prabhakar Vardhan, was the first of the Vardhana dynasty. His younger son was Harsha Vardhana. The elder son Rajya Vardhana ascended the throne after their father.

When his elder brother was deceived and murdered, Harsha swore revenge. He was only 16 at the time. He waged a battle against the King of Gauda, who was responsible for Rajya's death; and Harsha won.

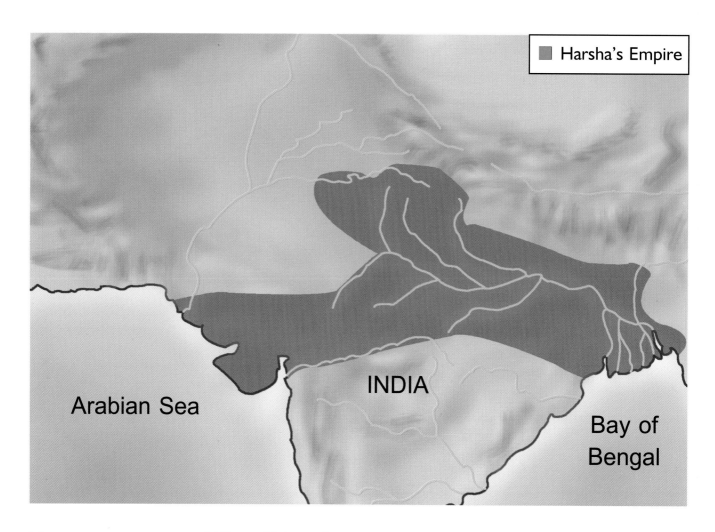

He was now crowned King. Although very young, Harsha proved himself to be a great conqueror and able administrator. His first move was to unite the two Kingdoms of Thanesar and Kannauj. He then brought Bengal, Bihar and Orissa under his control. He conquered Dhruvasena of Gujarat and later, married off his daughter to him. He also conquered Ganjam, a part of present-day Orissa.

Harsha's plan to conquer Southern India was stopped by Pulakesi II of Vatapi. Thus, the river Narmada was marked as the Southern limit of Harsha's Empire. Harsha went on to reunite the small republics from Punjab to Central India.

Harsha was a patron of art and literature. He even made several donations to the Nalanda University. Harsha himself was an author of merit, having written three Sanskrit plays 'Nagananda', 'Ratnavali' and 'Priyadarsika'. His court poet Bana-

Bhatta wrote the first historical poetic work on King Harsha, 'Harsha Charitam'. In it are listed all of the great King's exploits and achievements.

He was also a great patron of culture. His capital city, Kannauj, extended for four or five miles along the Ganges River and consisted of magnificent buildings. Only one fourth of the taxes he collected went to administration of the government. The remainder went to charity, rewards, and especially to further culture: art, literature, music, and religion. Trade too, flourished during this period.

Although a Shaivite himself, he was tolerant of all faiths; Buddhism, Hinduism and Jainism Sometime later in his life, he became a patron of Buddhism also. King Harsha Vardhana propagated the religion by constructing numerous stupas in the name of Buddha.

Harsha ruled wisely for 41 years. When he died, he left behind no heirs and so the

Stupas constructed by Harshavardhana

Kingdom disintegrated into smaller states once more.

Soon after, three dynasties fought for control of Northern India; the Pratiharas of Malwa, the Palas of Bengal and the Rashtrakutas of the Deccan.

With Harsha's death, the idea of a Northern Empire that panned the whole of India collapsed. The focus shifted to the South.

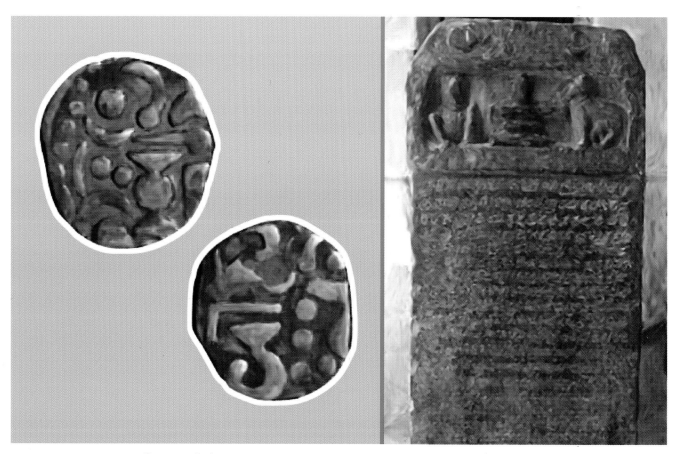

Coins - Palas   *Inscription - Rashtrakutas*

Chapter - 12

THE KINGDOMS OF THE DECCAN
The Chalukyas

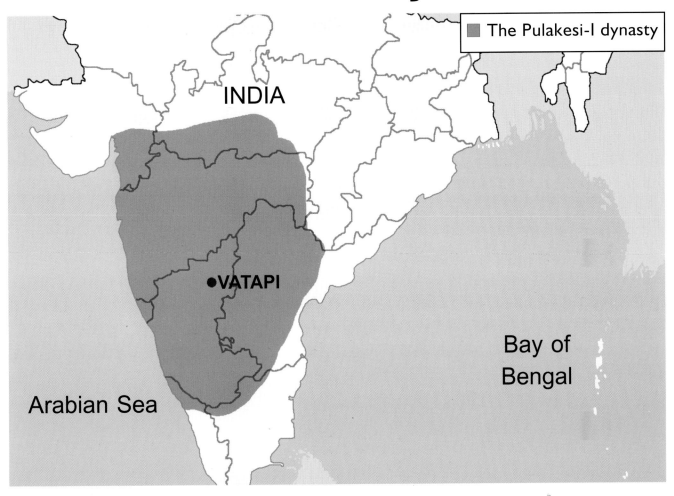

The dominant Empire in the Deccan region of India during the sixth and eighth Century was that of the Chalukyas.

There were three segragations of Chalukyas who ruled the Deccan, the early Chalukyas who ruled from the Badami region, the Eastern Chalukyas who ruled from the Vengi region and the Western Chalukyas who ruled from the Kalyani region.

The Badami Chalukyas were the earliest dynasty and are believed to be natives of Karnataka. They ruled from their capital at Vatapi. Pulakesi I was the first ruler of this dynasty. The Empire stretched over the entire State of Karnataka and most of Andhra Pradesh.

He was followed by the most prominent ruler of the Badami Chalukyas - Pulakesi II. Earlier known as Ereya, he ascended the throne in 608. He assumed control over the whole of the Deccan.

One of his famous conquests is the defeat of the Vishnukundins in Southeastern Deccan. He consolidated his Kingdom by conducting campaigns against the Alupas, Gangas and others. His two queens were Princesses from the Alupa dynasty and the Western Ganga dynasty. The Chalukyas always maintained close ties with these dynasties.

He clashed with the Pallava king, Mahendravarman, in Tamil Nadu Successfully and conquered his Kingdom.

The most famous conquest of Pulakesi II was the clash against Harshavardhana. He successfully stopped the King and prevented him from conquering lands

Pulakesi II and Harshavardhana fighting.

Pulakesi II and Harshavardhana signed a treaty.

further South. The two signed a treaty marking the river Narmada as the boundary between the Chalukya Empire and Harsha's Empire.

Now Pulakesi's control extended fully over the South, including Maharashtra. But now he had to stop his campaigns. His treasury was nearly empty from all the wars fought and expansion was put on hold. However, having conquered Southern India, Pulakesi acquired the title of Dakshinapatheshwara, meaning Lord of the South.

In 609, he appointed his brother Kubja Vishnuvardhana as the Viceroy of Vengi. Shortly thereafter Kubja declared his independence from Pulakesi and established the Eastern Chalukya Empire.

Pulakesi encouraged trade by sending emissaries to other countries. He sent

Pulakesi welcomed ambassadors from Persia. Hsuan Tsang

ambassadors to Persia and welcomed ambassadors from there. He was also a great admirer of art, literature and poetry. He encouraged every form of art in his Kingdom. The three prominent Kannada poets in his Kingdom were Adikavi Pampa, Sri Ponna and Ranna . Telegu literature too, progressed during this period under the Eastern Chalukyas.

Pulakesi was an able administrator and a wise King. His subjects revered him and were devoted to him. As noted by a Chinese traveller named Hsuan Tsang, Pulakesi had divided his Empire into three Maharashtrakas or great provinces. Each province covered 99,000 villages. It is estimated that his territory covered Karnataka, Maharashtra including coastal Konkan. These were further divided into Rashtrakas, Vishayas or districts and Bhogas (groups of ten villages).

Though he himself was a Hindu, Pulakesi was tolerant of Buddhism and Jainism as

The Virupaksha Temple   *The sculptures of Virupaksha Temple.*

well. He built many monasteries in his Kingdom that provided shelter to almost 5000 monks. It was a period of great peace and prosperity and riches. It was also a period of efficient administration, overseas trade and commerce.

The Chalukya dynasty as a whole was famous for encouraging art and architecture. A new style of architecture termed as the Chalukyan architecture was developed. Many temples were built near the Badami region. One famous example is the Virupaksha Temple in Karnataka. The sculptures of this temple are beautifully carved and sculpted. Every sculpture represents a scene from the epic 'Ramayana'. Some paintings from the Ajanta and Ellora caves too, are believed to belong to this era.

Pulakesi's clashes with the Pallava Empire continued on and off during his reign. In 642, Pulakesi met his match in the Pallava King, Narasimhavarman, and was defeated. Narasimhavarman occupied Badami temporarily. Pulakesi II, it is believed, died fighting, a hero till the last breath.

After the death of Pulakesi II, the Eastern Chalukyas became an independent Kingdom in Eastern Deccan. They ruled from the capital of Vengi until the eleventh Century.

The Badami Chalukyas were ousted by the Rashtrakutas, rulers of the Western Deccan. Badami was ruled by the Pallavas for a period of thirteen years. But the Chalukyas soon returned to prominence through their descendents, the Western Chalukyas. The latter ruled from Kalyani till the end of the 12th Century.

The Empire was strengthened under Vikramaditya I and II. The latter conquered many lands.

Badami Chalukya Temple

Vikramaditya VI   *Yadava coins*

The Western Chalukyas were in constant conflict with the Cholas. Vikramaditya VI was an ambitious and skilled military leader who led the Western Chalukyas to victory against the Chola influence in Vengi. This ruler was also known as Vikramanka and was the most famous ruler of the dynasty.

The death of Vikramanka marked the end of the Chalukya dynasty. In 1190, the Hoysalas and Yadavas took over the Empire.

Chapter - 13

The Pallavas

Pallava architecture at Mahabalipuram.

One of the most powerful dynasties to rule the Southern parts of India was the Pallava dynasty. Ruling for nearly 500 years, they were great conquerors and had a huge impact on art and architecture in the South.

Initially the Pallavas conquered the region of Thondaimandalam that was located in Pallavapuri. But a natural disaster occurred in the area and it was washed away by the sea. The Pallavas then moved further South to Kanchipuram and it was from here that the mighty empire was ruled. It extended from Northern Orissa to Tanjore and Trichi in the far South.

The first ruler of the Pallavas was believed to be Skandavarman, who ruled in the early fourth century. Skandavarman extended his territories from the Krishna in the North to the Pennar in the South, and to the Bellary district in the West. He performed the Ashwamedha and other Vedic sacrifices and earned the title of 'Supreme King of Kings devoted to Dharma'.

The Pallavas began to expand their Kingdom very fast and covered the areas of North and South Arcot, Chengalpet and a part of Tanjore. More than sixteen Kings ruled between 350 and 575. Sambavishnu, who ruled from 560 to 580, was a strong ruler who defeated the Cholas, Pandyas and Kalabhras, the ancient dynasties that ruled the Southern regions. The ruler was a devotee of Lord Vishnu. At the Adi Varaha temple of Mahabalipuram in Tamil Nadu, a portrait of this King and his Queen is displayed.

Next in line was his son, Mahendravarman, who ruled from 600 to 630. He was an able and skillful ruler. Conflicts with the Chalukyas of Badami started during his reign and continued for centuries.

Rock temple - Mahabalipuram

Mahendravarman was a learned man and a skillful poet and musician as well. He was adept at playing the musical instrument, veena. Music, dance, art and architecture flourished under his rule. The work on the magnificent cave temples of Mahabalipuram near Chennai were started by this great King.

But the peace and prosperity did not last. The Chalukya King, Pulakesi II, heard of the riches of Kanchipuram and decided to invade the Pallava Empire. He attacked the army of Mahendravarman at Pullalar in the year 620. The Pallavas suffered a defeat and Mahendravarman was shattered. The humiliated Mahendravarman was never the same again and his health took a turn for the worse.

He bravely tried to seek revenge by challenging Pulakesi in a series of battles in the Northern region of Tamil Nadu. But he did not succeed. Finally, he died a broken man in the year 630.

Mahendravarman died a broken man in the year 630.

Pulakesi II defeated by Narasimhavarman.

Mahendravarman's son, Narasimhavarman, was a man of great intelligence and courage. He swore to avenge his father's humiliation.

He challenged Pulakesi II to a battle at Manimangalam and later at Pariyalam in 632.

Both times, Pulakesi II was defeated and Narasimhavarman emerged victorious. He had achieved what his father could not. Pulakesi II was forced to retreat and agreed not to conquer lands further South.

Narasimhavarman now assumed control of Badami and the Pallavas ruled this land for thirteen years. The King had a powerful navy and with this, he helped the King of Simhala (Sri Lanka) to regain his lost Kingdom.

The Kailasanatha temple at Kanchipuram.

Narasimhavarman completed the beautiful cave temples at Mahabalipuram. These rock-cut temples have magnificent pillared halls and monolithic shrines or rathas.

He also built a host of other temples like the Kailasanatha temple at Kanchipuram and the Shore Temple. The King was a wrestler and had earned the title 'Mamalla', the great wrestler, which is probably the reason why Mahabalipuram is also known as Mamallapuram.

Though the Pallava Kings were Brahmins , they allowed the freedom of religion in their Kingdom. Many practiced Buddhism and there were at least 10,000 Buddhist monks at Kanchipuram at the time. One of the greatest scholars of the time was Dharmapala and he hailed from this capital city. He was president of the Nalanda University.

Sculptures of the Vaikunta Perumal.   *Sculpture of Rajasimha Narasimhavarman.*

After Narasimhavarman, came six more Kings, Pallavamalla Nandivarman being one of the most successful. Since Narasimhavarman had no direct descendant, Nandivarman was chosen to succeed him. Nandivarman was a descendant of Simha Vishnu's (one of the early Pallava rulers) brother.

Between 700 and 728, there was a period of peace and prosperity under the reign of Rajasimha Narasimhavarman II. Art and literature flourished. The famous Sanskrit writer Dandin was his court poet. The lovely sculptures of the Vaikuntha Perumal temple of Kanchipuram were built during this period. The period also saw the beginning of trade with China.

While art and architecture was booming, the conflicts with the Chalukyas of Badami and the Tamil Kingdoms of the Cholas and Pandyas in the South continued. Finally, during the eighth century, Vijayalaya, the Chola King, defeated the last Pallava King Aparajitavarma. And thus ended the rule of the Pallavas.

Chapter - 14

The Cholas

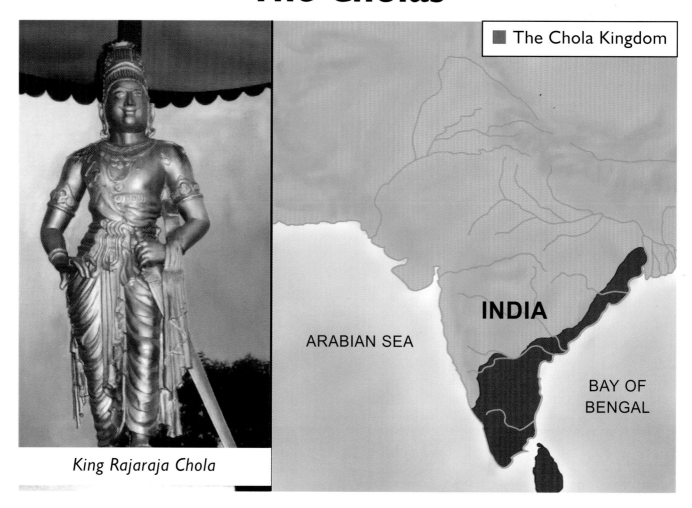

King Rajaraja Chola

The Chola Kingdom

INDIA

ARABIAN SEA

BAY OF BENGAL

By the 8th century, the three prominent Kingdoms of the South were those of the Cholas, the Cheras and the Pandyas.

Believed to have originated from the fertile valley of the river Kaveri, the Cholas were the most powerful of the three.

Following the death of King Vijayalaya who defeated the Pallavas, his successors, Aditya Chola and Parantaka took over the reins of the Kingdom. Tanjore was the capital of the Chola Kingdom.

The year 985 saw one of the greatest Kings of Southern India ascend the throne. He was Rajaraja Chola I. The King, who was also known as Rajaraja, the Great,

Tanjore temple

defeated the Eastern Chalukyas of Vengi, the Pandyas of Madurai and the Gangas of Mysore.

His campaign of expansion included the capture of Sri Lanka, which remained under Chola rule for another 75 years. He conquered the islands of the Maldives and even sent missions to Indonesia.

Both, an able administrator and a great lover of architecture, he commissioned the building of a magnificent temple at Tanjore. The temple is named 'Rajarajeshwar' after him.

Rajendra Chola, the heir and son of Rajaraja Chola I, who took over the Kingdom after the latter's death was an able ruler, just like his father. His greatest achievement included the conquest of the Andaman and Nicobar islands. Rajendra appointed his son as the first Chola-Pandya Viceroy Prince in Madurai.

Tanjore - Inside of a Temple

The King now attacked the Western Chalukyas and their allies. He conquered lands up to the banks of the river Ganga. From the holy river, he collected the sacred water in golden pots and poured it into a tank he called Chola Ganga. He then adopted the title of Gangaikonda which means Victor of the Ganga.

The period under his reign, came to be known as the Golden Age of the Cholas. Art, music, dance, poetry, drama, arts, sculpture, painting, philosophy and religion, all reached new heights. The temple was the center of all activity. It was almost like an institution. The temple courtyard was like a school where students were taught the ancient Vedas and scriptures. Temples were built like citadels where people could seek shelter during an emergency.

It was a time of religion and the worship of Lord Shiva increased. The language of Tamil received great encouragement and many beautiful works of Tamil literature are attributed to this period. The famous poet Kamban lived during this period and his work 'Ramavatharam' is one of the greatest epics of Tamil literature. Jayamkondar's masterpiece 'Kalingattuparani' is another example of narrative poetry depicting the Kalinga War of the Cholas.

The Cholas also laid a much emphasis on architecture. Magnificent temples were built and the Brihadiswara temple at Tanjore is a prime example. Another famed art form were the bronze statues carved at the time. Intricately carved and detailed with jewellery and garlands, these statues are a testimony to the talented craftsmen of the Chola dynasty. The Nataraja and the Ardhanarishwara are famous examples of this art form.

The Cholas became the most prominent artistic, cultural, religious and political force in the South. The Empire was divided into mandalams or provinces. These

Statue of Nataraja.   *Statue of Ardhanarishwara.*

Rajendra Chola's daughter was married to the Chalukya prince, Vimaladitya.

were divided further into Valanadus and Nadus.

Following Rajendra's rule, three of his sons and one grandson succeeded him. Thereafter, a new line of Chalukya-Cholas ascended the throne. The Eastern Chalukyas and the Cholas had inter-married through the generations and thus the new clan was born. Rajendra Chola's daughter was married to the Chalukya Prince, Vimaladitya.

One of the Chalukya-Chola rulers was Rajendra II, an Eastern Chalukyan prince, who called himself 'Kulottunga' or 'Star of the Dynasty'. Under his rule, Sri Lanka gained independence from Chola Rule. His reign was one of peace and prosperity. Trade with Southeast Asia flourished, with many diplomatic missions sent to China. Around the year 1118, they lost control of Vengi to the Western Chalukya king, Vikramaditya VI.

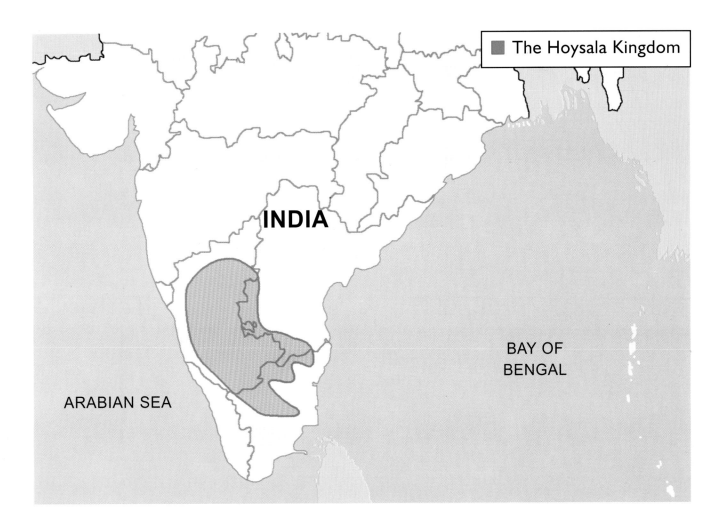

The future Chola Kings all faced trouble in one way or the other. As the Northern Chalukyas were being replaced by the Hoysalas, the Cholas too, were becoming weaker. They were constantly assaulted.

By the thirteenth century, the Pandyan monarchs were gaining strength. The Chola Empire shrank to the region around Tanjore and soon came to an end when the last Chola King, Rajaraja III died.

Chapter - 15

The Cheras

Utiyan Cheralatan defeated by a Chola ruler.

The Chera Kingdom was located to the South of the Mauryan Empire. Their land included the Malabar Coast, Karur, Coimbatore and Salem Districts in South India. These are now part of Kerala and Tamil Nadu. The Chera capital was Tiruvanchikulam.

The first Chera King was Utiyan Cheralatan, who is said to have founded the dynasty. Once he fought against a Chola ruler and suffered a humiliating defeat. Unable to bear this insult, Utiyan Cheralatan committed suicide.

He was followed by his son Imayavaramban Nedun Cheralatan, who was responsible for making the Cheras one of the powerful dynasties in the South. During his rule of 58 years, this King won many wars with a major victory being against his sworn enemies, the Kadambas of Banavasi.

He not only extended the Kingdom, but also enhanced it culturally. During his reign, art and literature flourished. His court boasted of the famous poet, Kannanar.

The greatest Chera King is said to be Kadalpirakottiya Vel Kelu Kuttuvan. It is said that the great Tamil epic 'Silappadigaram', which describes a mythical hero, refers to him. Silappadigaram, meaning 'The Jewelled Anklet', is one of the three great Tamil epics of the era, the other two being 'Manimegalai' and 'Sivagami-Sindamani'.

Kuttavan is said to have achieved triumphant victories at Mogur Mannan and Kongar. He also established the Patni (wife) cult, which stresses on the wife's devotion to her husband. A famous example of this is the story of the faithful

Statue of Kannagi   The Jewelled Anklet

77

Statue of the Alwars.

woman that is still remembered today - Kannagi.

The Chera Kings were constantly in conflict with the neighbouring Kingdoms to establish their power. They also married into other clans to strengthen their positions. The Kingdom prospered greatly and a strong overseas trade links were established, especially with Rome. They traded in spices, ivory and sandalwood. They also exported pearls and gems to the Middle East. This was one way which spread Judaism.

Then came a dark age, where the Cheras were eclipsed by the Kalabhras. When they were overthrown, the second Chera Empire came into existence, with Mahodyapuram as its capital. It was founded by Kulasekhara Alvar. He was one of the 12 Alvars or Tamil saints who composed songs and sang hymns in praise of

Trade between Kerala and China.

Lord Vishnu. The Alvars established the Bhakti (devotional) cult in South India.

Kulasekhara was a scholar and a great lover of art. He composed five dramas; 'Perumal Tirumozhi', 'Mukundamala', 'Tapatisamvarna', 'Subhadradhamala' and 'Vichchinnabhiseka'.

His successor was Rajasekhara Varman Rul, who founded the Killam Era in Kerala. He was followed by Sthanu Ravi Varman, who is said to have been on friendly terms with the Chola monarchs. During his reign there was a flourishing trade between Kerala and China.

But upon his death, the relationship between the Cheras and Cholas disintegrated. The last Chera King was Rama Varma Kulasekhara and when he shifted his capital to Quilon, the Cholas took over Mahodyapuram. When he died, it was the end of the Chera Empire.

Chapter - 16

The Pandyas

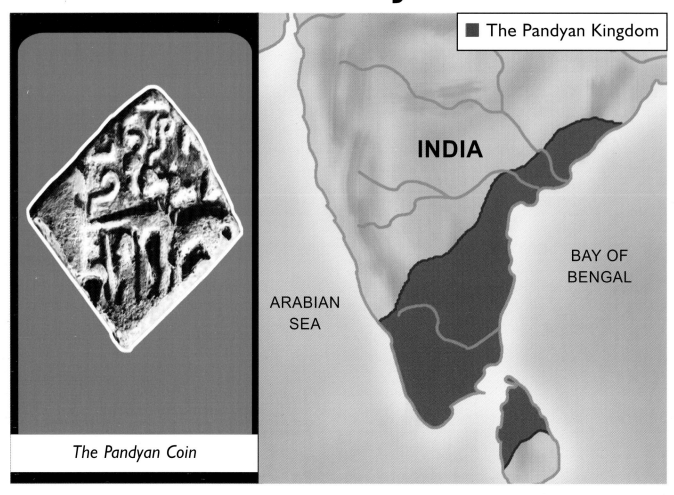

The Pandyan Coin

The Pandyan Kingdom was one of three ancient Kingdoms in South India. They ruled Tamil Nadu until the end of the fifteenth century.

Their capital was initially Korkai, a seaport on the Southernmost tip of India. Later the capital was moved to Madurai.

The first Pandyan Empire was established by the Emperor Kadungon in the sixth century. He ascended the throne after defeating the clan of Kalabhras.

The Pandyas grew in power and expanded their Empire. The entire Tamil country was divided between the Pallavas and Pandyas. The river Kaveri formed a boundary between the two Kingdoms.

Some of finest pearls were produced during the Pandyan period.

The Pandyas controlled the districts that are known today as Madurai and Tirunalveli as well as a part of Southern Kerala.

The Pandyas were famous for their extensive trade network. They even had contacts with Rome and Greece. They excelled at sea trade, especially through Dhanushkodi, the sea shore of Ramanathapuram, and Poompuhar, a city used for trade with China, Malaysia, the Maldives and others. They controlled the pearl fisheries along the South Indian coast between Sri Lanka and India. They produced some of the finest pearls known.

Even though it was a powerful Kingdom in its own way, the Pandyan Kingdom was often subdued during clashes with the Pallavas and Cholas. This happened as their Kingdom expanded and their neighbours, feeling threatened by them, attacked.

Soon, the Pandyas were overshadowed by the Cholas. This happened during the rule of Parantaka Chola II. His son, Aditya Karikala led a massive army in a war against Vira Pandya and defeated him. The Sinhalese forces (Sri Lankans) came to the Pandyas' rescue but to no avail. The Pandyan Kings were driven out of their territories and who then sought refuge in Sri Lanka. With this started a long period of exile for the Pandyas.

Taking over their Kingdom were the Cholas Viceroys who called themselves Chola Pandyas and ruled from Madurai from 1020 AD.

However, in the thirteenth century the Chola power began to decline. Once again the Pandyas emerged from hiding and expanded their territory from the Telegu lands by the Godavari to the Northern half of Sri Lanka. The Cholas had become weak and were fast losing control of their lands.

The two famous Pandyan Kings who revived the glory of the clan were Maravarman Sundara Pandya and his successor, the famous Jatavarman Sundara

Aditya Karikala led a massive army in a war against Vira Pandya and defeated him.

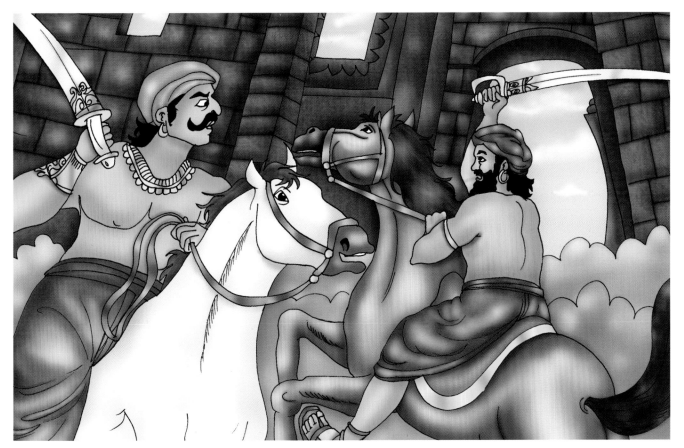

Sundara Pandya and Vira Pandya fought against each other for the throne.

Pandya. The latter was a brave and ambitious warrior King. His main goal was to subdue the Cholas completely. He fought many battles fiercely and managed to consolidate his hold over Trichi, Srirangam, Tanjore and Kumbakonam.

Another King, Maravarman Kulasekara Pandya I also tried to revive the Pandyan glory. But upon his death, his sons Sundara Pandya and Vira Pandya fought against each other for the throne. In this time of chaos, a general of the Delhi Sultanate, Malik Kafur, took advantage of the situation and raided the Kingdom. The Pandyan rule came to an abrupt end. Later on, the Pandyas were nothing more than local chieftains who owned some land around Tirunalveli.

Chapter - 17

The Rajputs

The Rajput people

During the 7th and 8th Century a clan of people emerged who called themselves Rajputs, meaning 'Sons of a King'. They belonged to the warrior class or Kshatriyas and hailed from Rajasthan and other parts of Central India. The Rajputs belonged to three kinds of Vanshas or ancestries; Suryavanshi, Chandravanshi and Agnivanshi. Under Agnivanshi are the clans of Pratiharas, Solankis, Paramaras and Chauhans. Among themselves, they established Kingdoms in Marwar, Ujjain, Malwa, Kannauj, Ajmer and Gujarat.

The Rajputs were known for their loyalty and fierce courage. Women were also trained in the art of war, and did not hesitate to go into the battlefield if their men were outnumbered. However, if the King and all his men were killed in a battle, the Rajput women preferred to commit suicide rather than allow themselves to be taken as prisoners. This ritual was known as 'Jauhar'.

Prithviraj Chauhan　　　　*A painting of Prithviraj and Princess Sanyogita.*

One of the most prominent Rajput ruler was Prithviraj Chauhan, born in 1168 AD to the King of Ajmer, Someshwar Chauhan. Adept at military tactics, he could hit a moving target by merely listening to the sound. When he was just 13, his father died and he ascended the throne. Prithviraj was a romantic, chivalrous and an extremely fearless person. His kidnapping of the Princess Sanyogita or Samyukta is legendary. She was the daughter of his enemy, Jayachandra of Kannauj, and she loved him as passionately as he loved her. Her father arranged her Swayamvara*, but did not invite Prithiviraj Chauhan. However, Prithiviraj bravely rode in, abducted her and sped away. Jayachandra's soldiers chased him, but could not catch him. He got away at last and married his beloved. The story is narrated in the epic poem 'Prithviraj Raso', composed by Prithviraj's court poet and friend, Chand Bardai.

In the meantime, he expanded his Empire further and controlled most of

* Marriage by choice

85

Rajasthan and Haryana and unified the Rajputs against Muslim invasion. In the meantime, a Muslim conqueror named Mohammad Shahab-ud-din Ghori was, capturing nearby Kingdoms in a well-planned military invasion. He captured provinces like Multan, Uchcha, Gujarat and Punjab. As he covered more areas, he became a threat to Prithviraj's territory.

Prithviraj started to prepare for war. The two clashed at the First Battle of Tarain, now in the Karnal district of Haryana. Prithiviraj defeated him with his massive army of loyal soldiers. As Ghori retreated, Prithviraj was advised to attack the retreating armies. The noble King refused, as it went against the Rajput code of conduct. This proved to be his undoing as Ghori soon came back with his armies for a second attack.

This time, during the Second Battle of Tarain, Prithviraj was defeated and captured. It is said that he was tortured and his eyes were pierced with red-hot

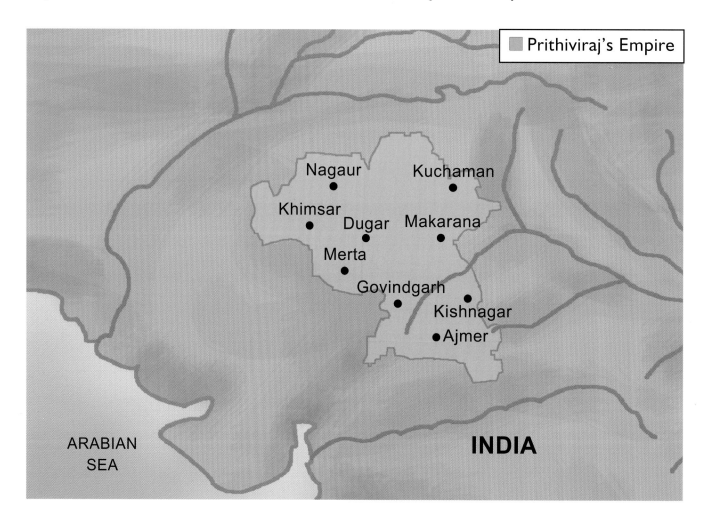

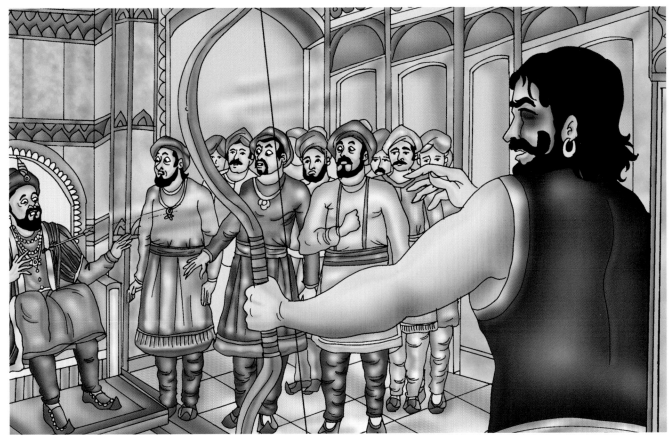

Prithviraj displays his skills and kills his enemy.

iron rods. Thereafter, in an archery contest, he displayed his archery skills by hitting targets in spite of being blinded. He did this without a single error and Ghori is said to have praised him for this feat. Hearing his voice, Prithviraj is believed to have aimed an arrow in his direction that killed his enemy. In 1192 AD, Prithviraj Chauhan died, ending an era of profound bravery, courage and morality.

Maharana Pratap, Bappa Rawal, Rana Sanga, Jaswant Singh and Rani Padmini have made an indelible mark on the pages of Indian History. Maharana Pratap, the ruler of Mewar, is synonymous with Rajput valour and chivalry. At a time when all the Rajput States were allying with Akbar, Mewar remained independent. Furious, Akbar attacked Mewar in the famous Battle of Haldighati. Pratap lost to Akbar but did not surrender and continued his combats till the end of his life. Gradually, the power of the Rajputs dwindled. They were no match for the Mughals who invaded later. When the British arrived in India, the Rajput States became colonies, thus ending the reign of the Rajputs forever.

Kerala, in coastal South India, was invaded by the Muslims from Arabia.

India's flourishing international trade, and reputation as the only known source of diamond mines in the world, attracted many invasions from outsiders. For centuries the North Indian Kingdoms resisted the invasions from Arab-Turks. But soon, small Islamic Empires or Sultanates were established in several parts of the North.

Even before that, Muslim trading communities existed in coastal South India, especially Kerala. They arrived here from Arabia in small numbers through the Indian Ocean.

Qutb-ud-din Aybak

In the twelfth and thirteenth centuries, the Arabs, Turks and Afghans invaded parts of North India and established the Delhi Sultanate in the former Rajput regions.

The establishment of the Sultanate led to a vast change in the culture. An Indo-Muslim culture evolved and its effects were seen in monuments, architecture, music, literature and religion. It is said that the language of Urdu was the result of a mix of Sanskrit and Persian, Turkish and Arabic. The Delhi Sultanate was the only Indo-Islamic Empire to place a woman on its throne, the famous Razia Sultan.

Qutb-ud-din Aybak, who was a general in Ghori's army, established the Delhi Sultanate. Later, Shams-ud-din Iltumish established a Turkish Kingdom in Delhi, which enabled the future Sultans to conquer Kingdoms in different directions. Over the next few centuries, the Delhi sultanate extended its way to Bengal and the Deccan.

In the meantime, a Turkish-Mongol conqueror named Timur launched a campaign to invade India. He attacked Sultan Nasir-ud-din Mehmud of the Tughlaq Dynasty at Delhi. The Sultan's armies were defeated. Timur entered Delhi and the city was destroyed and left in ruins.

With this, the Delhi Sultanate came to an end. Next came the Mughal Empire.

The founder of the Mughal Empire was Zahir-ud-din Muhammad Babur, a descendant of Timur and Genghis Khan. Muslim armies, comprising Mongol, Turkish, Persian and Pashtun warriors, invaded India under his leadership. In the legendary First Battle of Panipat in 1526, Babur defeated the last of the Delhi Sultans, Ibrahim Shah Lodhi. Though Babur had only 12,000 men, they were well trained. The Sultan had more than 100,000 men. But Babur had the advantages of superior cavalry tactics, firearms and guns. He was the first Mughal emperor.

Babur   *Humayun*

Humayun lived a life of luxury.

Babur went on to crush the Rajput, Rana Sanga of Chittor and achieved many other military victories. But just five years into his reign, he died. His biggest legacy was a set of descendants who fulfilled his dream of an Islamic Empire in India.

Babar's successor was his son, Humayun. At 12, his father had appointed him governor of Badakshan, where he proved his administrative skills and bravery.

However, when he ascended the throne, it was realized that he lacked his father's clever and crafty mind, even though he was a good soldier. He became addicted to the luxuries of the palace and did not take much action against the Rajputs and Afghan nobles who were conspiring against him.

His brothers too, were conspiring against him, but Humayun refused to believe it and gave them positions of power. One of his biggest threats was the Afghan general, Sher Shah Suri, who had served under Babur. Humayun thought Sher

Sher Shah Suri and his army

Shah had only a few tribesmen and no armies and so, he ignored him. In reality, Sher Shah had gathered an impressive number of Afghans who were all fiercely loyal and well trained. He continued to gather forces and expand his territory.

Humayun, finally understanding his threat, marched to Chunar, Sher Shah's territory, while the latter was away at Gaur. But, in spite of the absence of their leader, his men fought fiercely and Humayun had to retreat.

Sher Shah managed to capture the Mughal lands of Bihar and Jaunpur. A humiliated Humayun clashed with Sher Shah two more times. The first was at Chausa where he suffered a crushing defeat and barely escaped with his life. The next time was at Kannauj and this was the final blow. Humayun's reign was over and Sher Shah captured Delhi and Agra, establishing the Afghan rule.

Betrayed by his brothers, Humayun fled to Persia. For 15 years, he lived in exile. During this time, his wife gave birth to a son, Akbar.

After the death of Sher Shah Suri, the regime began to unravel as his successor was unable to recreate the magic of Sher Shah's rule.

On realizing this, Humayun gathered an army with the help of the then Persian King and marched towards Delhi. The next year, he captured Delhi, along with Kabul and Kandahar. His days of exile were over and he ascended the throne at Agra after the defeat of Sikander Suri, Sher Shah's successor.

A changed man, Humayun devoted himself to his State. His biggest achievement at this time was in the sphere of painting. He recruited several Persian painters to come to India and they laid the foundation for Mughal art and style that has gone down in history. From then on, there was a fusion of Persian and Indian styles.

Humayun sitting on the throne at Agra.

Humayun fell from his library steps and died on the spot.

But his reign was short-lived. In a tragic accident, he fell from his library steps and died on the spot. His son, Akbar, who went on to become one of the greatest Mughal Kings, succeeded him.

Akbar the Great

Akbar learnt to fight and hunt.

Jalaluddin Mohammad Akbar was born while his parents were in exile in Persia and thus grew up in the Afghan countryside. His whole youth was spent in learning to fight and hunt. He did not have any interest in learning to read or write. As it later turned out, he was the only Mughal Emperor who though was illiterate, had a great thirst for knowledge.

When Humayun died, Akbar was away with the military commander, Bairam Khan in Punjab, campaigning for his father. He was only 13 at the time. He was sent for and crowned King, hurriedly. Bairam Khan was made the Regent, as the boy was too young. On Akbar's behalf, Bairam Khan led many campaigns to expand the Kingdom. As soon as Akbar came of age, he used his own judgement and skills for leadership.

One of his enemies was waiting for an opportunity to defeat the teenager who ruled the Mughal Empire. Hemu, the Hindu minister of the Afghan Prince, Adil Shah, attacked the Kingdom of Delhi. Hemu emerged victorious and crowned himself ruler of Delhi.

A furious Akbar launched an attack in the Second Battle of Panipat. The two armies fought valiantly and it looked like the Mughals would lose. Just when Akbar was despairing, an arrow hit Hemu's eye and he fainted. His men thought he was dead and laid down their weapons and surrendered to Akbar.

Akbar became King once more.

As Akbar grew older, he continued to annex more lands to his Empire. In the North, Akbar had conquered the Indo-Ganges Basin, Kashmir and Afghanistan. Gujarat and Sind in the West, Bengal in the East and part of the Deccan that

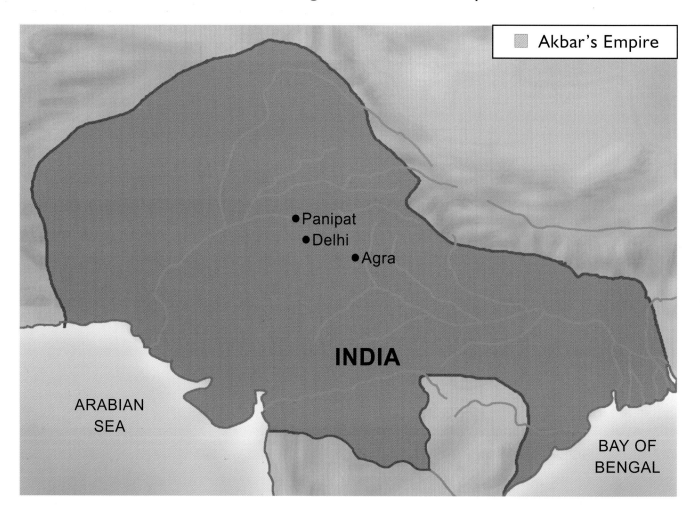

Akbar spoke to people of all religions.

Extended till the river Godavari in the South; he was King of all these lands very soon. Not much later, Bairam Khan betrayed Akbar. Bad advice made him revolt against Akbar and he was subsequently killed.

Although Akbar was still a very young Emperor, he was shrewd and organized. He got rid of all his ministers, as he knew they were too ambitious and would covet his position. He centralized the administration of his empire and ruled wisely.

He removed restrictions on religion and allowed his subjects to practice the religion of their choice, without fear of being persecuted.

His religious tolerance took him one step further. He had studied various religions and came up with the idea of merging the teachings of Islam, Hinduism, Christianity and Zorastrianism. Akbar poured a lot of energy into this new form of religion that he called Din-I-Ilahi or Divine Faith. He made himself the prophet or head of the religion.

Though he was keen on Din-I-Ilahi, the idea never took wing, mainly because the tenets of the new religion were not laid down clearly. Moreover, many considered this a threat to Islam.

In fact, even his half-brother Hakim, Governor of Kabul, rebelled against him. He felt Akbar was filling the people's minds with foolish notions and encouraging them to abolish Islam. Hakim sent a fatwa to all Muslims, urging them to revolt. But Akbar led an army against him and defeated him, thus taking over Kabul.

He solved the problem of rebellion from the Rajputs with a very simple policy. He gave the defeated Kings, positions of power and honour in his government and army. In fact, his first wife was a Rajput Princess, Jodha Bai. In this way, he

Akbar as the head of the religion.

Akbar was a master at riding, polo and swordsmanship.

encouraged Muslims to marry Rajputs. And that's why the Rajputs never rebelled against his rule like they did against other Mughal rulers.

Akbar was a master at riding, polo and swordsmanship. He was undeniably brave and a brilliant general.

He was fair to his subjects and abolished unfair taxes on non-Muslims. A number of social reforms also took place under his reign, like the abolishing of child marriage, the permission for widows to remarry and the removal of the ban on building new temples.

Although illiterate, he surrounded himself with scholars like Abul Fazl, Birbal and Tansen, who formed part of the Nine Gems or Navaratnas. These were the nine famous personalities from different walks of life. He always encouraged writers, musicians, painters and translators. He took keen interest in religion, philosophy, music, poetry, history and painting.

He had an impressive collection of books and manuscripts. He had the Hindu works like the 'Atharva Veda', the 'Ramayana' and the 'Mahabharata' translated.

Whichever city he ruled from, became the center for art, learning and culture. He encouraged Persian culture especially, and included a lot of its aspects in India.

One of his biggest accomplishments lies in his commitment to splendid architecture. Proof of this is the famous city of Fatehpur Sikri. It was named after his conquest of Gujarat. Situated 26 miles West of Agra, the royal city was his new capital and had elaborate palaces, sprawling courtyards, beautiful pools, tombs and a famous mosque. Spread over a length of two miles, the city was constructed

Akbar had many musicians in his court.

Akbar's crowning architectural achievement was the Jama Masjid at Agra.

from red sandstone by a large group of masons and stone carvers who were given a free hand to build. The style that evolved is known as Akbari.

A fabulous palace was built for Jodha Bai. Near this palace was the famous Hawa Mahal or the Palace of Winds. This palace overlooked beautiful gardens laid out in a distinct style.

Another of his crowning architectural achievements was the mosque - Jama Masjid. A huge courtyard was built for the congregation and the Stone-cutters' Mosque, one of the oldest places of worship at Sikri.

The architecture of the whole site was a blend of Hindu and Muslim styles. The entire palace complex was adorned with exquisite carvings, lattice and pierced stone screens, wall paintings, canopied roofs, carved brackets and pilasters.

Akbar's tomb

Akbar had three sons, Jahangir (also known as Salim), Murad and Daniyal. The last two died very early and only Jahangir survived. The father and son were constantly at conflict and disagreed on many things.

In 1605, Akbar fell seriously ill and died a slow death. His forty-year reign brought the East, West, North and Central India, along with parts of the South under one Empire. His rule was a glorious one and besides, the wealth of learning and culture that existed during the time is immensely valuable. He was also much admired for his bravery and wisdom.

Chapter - 20

Jahangir

A painting of Jahangir.   *Jahangir leading an army of 12000 men*

Akbar and his beloved wife Jodha, had a son after losing many children in infancy. He was named Nuruddin Salim Jahangir. Two more sons Murad and Daniyal were born shortly thereafter.

Jahangir was a great favourite in his father's court, thanks to his military skills and intelligence. His very first triumph was at the young age of 12, when he led a regiment of soldiers in Kabul and emerged the victor. At 16, he was made Mansabdar, which was a high military post, commanding 12000 men.

But the peace did not last long for Akbar and Jahangir started to disagree on many issues. Jahangir was jealous of the attention his father paid to his favourite scholar, Abul Fazl. The young Prince soon developed bad habits and began to drink heavily.

By this time, he was married and had children, one of them being the future ruler, Khurram. This child became Akbar's favourite grandchild and this too, bothered Jahangir. He was afraid that his father would favour Khurram over his eldest child Khusrau, who was the rightful heir.

After a series of misunderstandings with his father, Jahangir finally marched to Allahabad. Here, he declared himself King. A furious Akbar cut off all ties with him. Influenced by his friends, Jahangir blamed Abul Fazl for his father's hostility and ordered the scholar be killed. Akbar was shattered by his friend's death.

Finally, father and son came to their senses and were reunited. Akbar declared him his heir. Before Akbar died, he placed the crown on Jahangir's head.

Although Jahangir had led an irresponsible life earlier, he now ruled wisely and well. He followed a policy of expansion and crushed several rebellions against the

Akbar and Jahangir were reunited.

The Golden Chain of justice at the castle in Agra.

Mughal rule. He also released several prisoners of war. He was a great patron of art and learning.

One of his best measures to uphold justice was the Golden Chain of Justice. Sixty bells were connected by a chain, which hung outside the castle in Agra. Anyone with a grievance could pull the chain and be admitted to see the Emperor.

Jahangir was very tolerant of other religions like his father; especially because his own mother was a Hindu Rajput Princess.

One of the wives of Jahangir was Mehrunnisa, the wife of a slain rebel officer. He was captivated by her beauty and named her Nur Jahan, meaning 'Light of the World'. She involved herself in important matters of the State and her stepson Khurram was always in conflict with her.

Shalimar Bagh at the Dal Lake in Kashmir.

The good times did not last long. A ruler named Mahabat Khan attacked Jahangir's army and captured him. Thanks to Nur's plan, the Mughal King escaped. But it had taken a toll on his health, which had already deteriorated from excessive drinking. Jahangir now travelled to Kashmir to recover. Here, he found the peace he so desired. It was in Kashmir's Dal Lake that he built the magnificent Shalimar Bagh for his wife. It was a sprawling garden with a number of terraces linked by a water channel. Three lovely pavilions were built with black marble pillars and big halls.

Finally in 1627, Jahangir breathed his last. His son, Khurram marched to Agra and took over the reins of the Kingdom, imprisoning his stepmother, Nur Jahan in a beautiful mansion.

Chapter - 21

Shah Jahan

Shah Jahan spotted a beautiful girl in the market.

Shah Jahan or Khurram as he was named at birth, is most remembered for his incredible contribution to the Seven Wonders of the World, the Taj Mahal.

Even though he was the fifth child of Jahangir, he made his presence felt through his fighting skills and training. His father often sent him, even as a young child, on military campaigns.

Thanks to his numerous victories, Jahangir conferred the title of Shah Jahan or 'King of the World', on him.

When he was a mere fifteen years old, the young Prince was walking in a bazaar where he spotted a beautiful young girl, Arjumand Banu. Instantly enchanted by her beauty, Shah Jahan begged his father to allow him to marry her. But Jahangir refused, rubbishing his 'love story' and Shah Jahan was married off to a Persian Princess.

But he never forgot his first love. He courted her for five years until his father gave in. The two were finally married. The couple had fourteen children together, one of them being the future King, Aurangazeb.

In a few years, Jahangir's health deteriorated and his sons fought over the throne, until Shah Jahan took over. When he ascended the throne he gave his wife a new title Mumtaz Mahal or 'The Chosen One of the Palace'.

Shah Jahan's reign was happy and prosperous. It was an era of riches and the most precious gems were mined from India's soil and there were literally trunks and trunks of emeralds, sapphires, rubies, diamonds and all sorts of other treasures.

Shah Jahan giving away his treasure to the public.

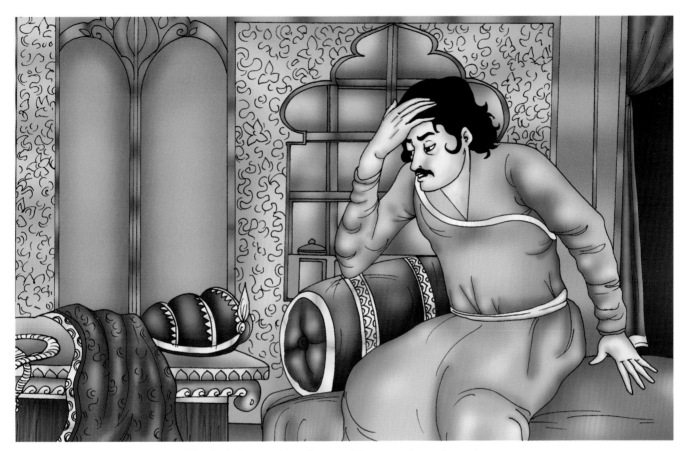

Shah Jahan shut himself up in his chambers.

Shah Jahan was immensely wealthy and built many palaces and mosques across the country. In fact, an inscription in gold on his throne says 'If there be a paradise on Earth, it is here'.

But tragedy awaited the Kingdom. In the fourth year of his reign, he set off for Burhanpur to quell a rebellion. Mumtaz, who was pregnant with their fourteenth child, insisted on going along. But while they camped at Burhanpur, she died after giving birth to a baby girl.

Shah Jahan was devastated. His grief and sorrow knew no bounds. He returned home, put aside his royal robes and shut himself up in his chambers. He refused to appear in public or take care of the State affairs.

For two years, he stayed this way, showing no interest in ruling his Empire. His only solace was in architecture and art.

Finally, one day he decided that he would build a beautiful monument of his love for his dead wife, such that had never been built before and never would again.

Thus, began his dream of building the Taj Mahal, the jewel of India. The foundation was laid on the banks of the river Yamuna, near his palace in Agra. It is said that three architects from Persia, Italy and France designed it. Skilled artisans were apparently brought from Baghdad, Constantinople and other Islamic centres.

The mausoleum took almost 20 odd years to build, with 20,000 men working hard day and night. The whole structure was made of marble brought from Jaipur and other precious metals and stones. The Taj stood majestically upon a platform, flanked on either side by beautiful mosques and minarets and a huge spired dome for a roof. Lush gardens with fountains spread almost to the foot of the Taj and a pool strategically placed in front of the monument reflected its shimmering

The Taj Mahal

Shah Jahan near the tomb of Mumtaz Mahal in the Taj Mahal.

beauty. Dazzling gems were inlaid in white marble with quotations from the Quran inscribed on the main entrance.

And within all this splendour lay the tomb of Mumtaz Mahal. Delicate screens surrounded her tomb, where light filtered through, giving it a dream-like quality.

Shah Jahan finally found peace here. His next plan was to build a black Taj Mahal across the river with a bridge connecting the two monuments. He wished that he would be laid to rest here, but that plan never materialised.

Years passed in this manner, and his peacefull life came to an end. He fell ill and his four sons started quarrelling over the throne. There were bitter fights, and Aurangzeb emerged victorious.

Shah Jahan could see the Taj Mahal from his chamber in Agra Fort.

He overthrew his father and placed him under house arrest. Shah Jahan's only desire was to see the Taj Mahal every day. Accordingly, he was moved to the Agra Fort where he lay in a chamber that offered a view of the monument.

For nine years he lay there, looked after by his daughter, Jahanara, and every living moment, he would gaze at the Taj and remember the days of love and joy.

Finally, old age and sickness overcame him and he breathed his last. According to his wishes, he was buried alongside Mumtaz inside the Taj. Their love became immortal and still lives on in the lovely stones of the Taj Mahal.

Chapter - 22

Aurangzeb

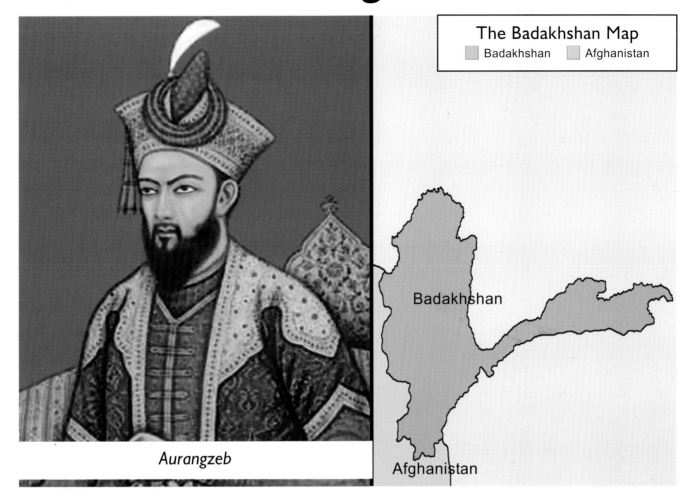

Aurangzeb

The Badakhshan Map

Badakhshan   Afghanistan

Badakhshan

Afghanistan

Aurangzeb is considered the last great Mughal ruler.

Born in 1618, he was the third son of Shah Jahan and Mumtaz Mahal. When he was only 16, his father gave him the post of the governor of Deccan. He moved to Kirki, which he renamed, Aurangabad.

In 1637, he married Rabia Durrani. In the meantime, Shah Jahan began to favour his eldest son, Dara Shikoh.

Aurangzeb soon earned his father's disfavour and was dismissed from his post. But soon after, he was made governor of Gujarat, where he performed well and was rewarded. By 1647, he was governor of Balkh and Badakhshan (present-day

Afghanistan and Tajikistan), replacing his ineffective brother, Murad Baksh.

These areas had been under attack from rebels for a while and Aurangzeb quelled them with his military skills. When he was appointed governor of Multan and Sindh, he began a long battle in an effort to capture Kandahar from the Safavid army. But he failed and once again earned his father's anger.

In 1652, he was once again appointed the Deccan governor. He began an intense campaign to expand the Mughal Empire but was stopped by his father and eldest brother every time.

Six years later, when Shah Jahan fell ill, the sons began to fight over the throne. Aurangzeb defeated his elder brother Dara's armies and took their father prisoner. Dara was condemned to death by his own brother.

Aurangzeb defeated his brothers and ascended the throne.

Aurangzeb's army consisted of many camp followers and camels.

The other brothers too, were defeated by Aurangzeb and he took over the throne at Agra . Now began Aurangzeb's rule that lasted forty-nine years.

Although the earlier Mughal Kings were tolerant of other religions, Aurangzeb was different. He enforced a strict Islamic law called the Fatwa-e-Alamgiri. Under this, he banned music and dance from his court. He also ordered the destruction of images in art and architecture, as Muslim Law dictates. He destroyed many Hindu temples, prohibited religious meetings and enforced the Jizya tax on non-Muslims, which Akbar had removed. He also banned Sati or the practice of forcing the widow to climb the funeral pyre of her husband. He forced many to convert to Islam as well.

Aurangzeb also began his earlier dream of expanding the Kingdom. He extended the Mughal territories both in the Northwest and Northeast. Aurangzeb's massive army consisted of some 500,000 camp followers, 50,000 camels, and

A Kashmir Brahmin seeking help from Tegh Bahadur.

30,000 war elephants. He pushed into Punjab and Afghanistan and also tried to suppress territories owned by the Marathas in the West, who were led by Chhatrapati Shivaji. But the constant military campaigns were a drain on the treasury. As a result, the peasants of the Kingdom had to pay heavy taxes.

Thanks to his restrictive rule, he had many enemies, especially the Sikhs. When Aurangzeb insisted that all Kashmir Brahmins be converted to Islam, the hapless Kashmiris turned to the Sikh Guru, Tegh Bahadur, for help. But Aurangzeb refused to listen to his pleas and instead, insisted that Tegh Bahadur himself convert to Islam. Upon his refusal, the Mughal had him executed. This triggered an open rebellion from the Sikhs.

Aurangzeb's army continued to weaken under constant attacks. It was at this time that his new enemies, the Marathas, attacked him. The struggle with them lasted

27 years. It was only when their leader, Shivaji died in 1680, that there was a respite.

But the relief was short-lived. The Rajputs of Jodhpur and Mewar joined forces and rebelled against Aurangzeb. They declared themselves independent of his rule. Aurangzeb sent his son, Akbar to quell their rebellion; not knowing that the latter would deceive him. Akbar declared himself King and soon had to flee to the Deccan where he allied with Shivaji's son, Sambhaji. Aurangzeb then drove his own son into exile in Persia, from where he never returned. Later, Aurangzeb caught and killed Sambhaji and stopped his forces.

But the decline of the Empire had begun. Aurangzeb's political power was weak, thanks to his complete focus on military matters. His provincial governors and generals became powerful and many declared themselves independent rulers. Moreover, his harsh rule had alienated the Hindus and the peasants, who lived in

Aurangzeb captured Sambhaji.

Maharaja Ranjit Singh

The Mughal Empire 1857

Lahore

Delhi

Agra

Rajashtan

Gujarat INDIA

Golkonda

Deccan

ARABIAN SEA

BAY OF BENGAL

utter poverty.

Shortly after his death in 1707, the Mughal Empire ceased to be an effective force in India. But it officially came to an end in 1857 when Emperor Bahadur Shah Zafar was put on trial. It was then that Mughal Empire was completely wiped out.

The Sikhs established their Empire in the Punjab after the death of Aurangzeb. Charat Singh, who was the head of one of the Sikh Clans, established his stronghold in Gujranwala in 1763. Maharaja Ranjit Singh was the most powerful of all the Sikh rulers and ruled for over 40 years. Ranjit Singh was also known as 'The Lion of Punjab'. He died of paralysis in 1839. After his death the Sikh Empire was divided into small principalities looked after by several Sikh Jagirdars.

Chapter - 23

The Rise of the Marathas

The Marathas

The rise of the Marathas was the main cause for the decline of the Mughals. The Marathas were an Indo-Aryan race who hailed from the present-day State of Maharashtra.

The Marathas were in power from 1674 to 1818 and during the peak of the Maratha rule, covered a territory of around 250 million acres. The Marathas were skillful warriors and were fiercely possessive about their land.

The origins of the Marathas can be traced back to an Ahmednagar general named Shahaji, a Hindu Maratha. This was the time of Shah Jahan, when the Deccan was controlled by the three Muslim Kingdoms of Ahmednagar, Bijapur and Golconda. The first was divided and large portions went to the Mughals and the balance to

Bijapur. Shahaji joined the Bijapur court. He sent his wife and son, Shivaji to Pune to look after his area.

From a young age, Shivaji heard tales of courage and valour from his mother, Jijabai. She taught him that they belonged to a race that was noble and brave; that they were meant to be Kings.

Shivaji grew up dreaming about an ideal nation. When he was just sixteen, he swore that one day he would establish a Hindu State and rule it.

Very soon, he had gathered a band of fiercely loyal Maratha men and set about conquering the nearby lands. Their first triumph was the mountain fort of Torna, near present-day Pune. Shivaji proclaimed himself governor. Knowing that he would face the wrath of the Bijapur Sultan, Muhammad Adil Shah, he wrote him a message. The message convinced him that Shivaji had taken over Torna in the

The Maratha King Shivaji.

120

People praising Shivaji.

Sultan's best interest as the people had not been paying their taxes. The unsuspecting Sultan accepted that and the group continued to conquer areas along the Western Ghats and the Konkan coast, using what is known as guerilla warfare.

Shivaji's fighting skills and courage soon won the love of the common people. When the Sultan realized he was becoming dangerously popular, he sent him a warning. But, by then it was too late. Shivaji had the backing of the common people.

Shivaji now wanted to expand his Empire. The alarmed Sultan sent his clever general, Afzal Khan to curb the activities of Shivaji. Knowing that Shivaji was very crafty himself, the general decided to trick Shivaji and then kill him. Leading an army of 40,000, the general marched off.

When Shivaji heard of his arrival, he sent a message requesting the general to meet him alone. Gleeful that an opportunity to kill Shivaji had presented itself, Afzal Khan agreed. He hid a dagger in his clothes and went to meet him. When he saw Shivaji, he embraced him, intending to stab and kill him. But before he could make the move, Shivaji made his. With tiger claws attached to his fingers, he dug them into Afzal Khan's stomach and killed him first.

Afzal's army was defeated. This was said to be the beginning of the mighty Maratha power.

When the Sultan of Bijapur died in 1656, Shivaji seized the opportunity to expand his Empire. He went on to conquer a number of hill forts near Pune. Very soon he had a large army and navy. He built many new forts and renovated several others.

He was a fair and just ruler and never differentiated in terms of religion or caste in his army. Everybody was equal.

Shivaji attacking Afzal Khan with tiger claws.

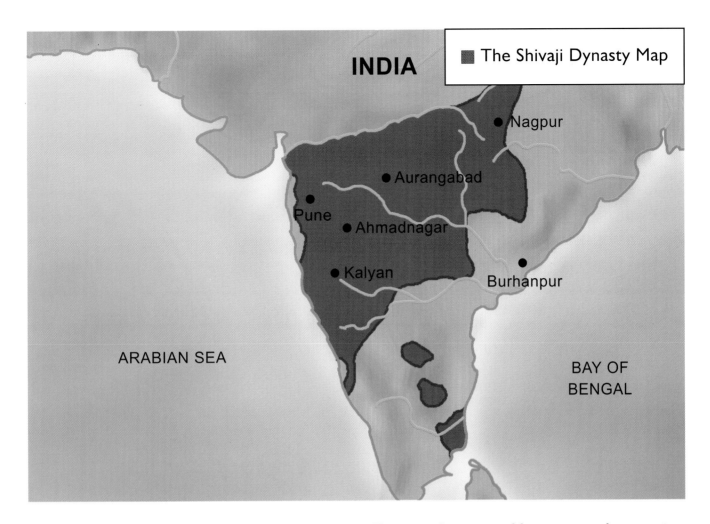

He appointed ministers who handled different divisions like internal security, foreign affairs, finance, law and justice, religious matters and defense. Everything was well organized in his administration.

He also introduced new systems in revenue collection. He reduced the power of the local landlords too, severely punishing those officials who harassed the people. His small Kingdom came to be known as Hindavi Swarajya (Sovereign Hindu State). At last, his dream was being realized. His Empire now stretched from Attock in Northwest India (now in Pakistan) to beyond Cuttack in East India.

He was fiercely patriotic and encouraged his people to fight against the tyranny of the Mughals.

The Mughal ruler, Aurangzeb had been watching his progress. He sent his uncle, Shaista Khan with a large army. Shivaji lost a large number of forts and areas to

Shivaji managed to escape in a basket of sweets.

Aurangzeb and was driven out of Pune. But he did not stay defeated for long. He soon overthrew Khan and re-established his rule. In a few years, he had recovered most of his lost forts.

In 1664, Shivaji set off on the daring mission of conquering Surat, a port city of rich traditions and great wealth and which was controlled by Aurangzeb. He took over the city and a furious Aurangzeb sent his general Jai Singh with a large army. After fighting for a long time, Shivaji surrendered and asked to see the Mughal ruler.

At his court, Aurangzeb ordered Shivaji to be thrown in prison. But he cleverly managed to escape in an enormous basket of sweets that were being distributed to religious leaders and poor people in the city.

After returning to Pune, he gathered his armies, attacked Jai Singh's troops that were retreating from Surat, and defeated them. During a short span after his return, Shivaji recaptured his forts and lands and re-established his Kingdom.

Chapter - 24

The Glory of Maratha Rule

Shivaji crowned the Maratha Emperor.

In 1674, Shivaji was crowned Emperor of the Maratha Empire. He came to be known as Chhatrapati Shivaji. This means 'Lord of the Universe'.

The coronation was a grand affair, with 11,000 Brahmins chanting the Vedas and 50,000 spectators watching awe-struck. Magnificent gifts were given to holy men and the poor.

Aurangzeb continued to send troops against him but Shivaji managed to expand Maratha control throughout the Deccan. Mughal efforts to take over the Deccan failed repeatedly.

Shivaji now had power over a vast area. He attacked Mughal camps in Berar and

Khandesh. He then set off towards the South and conquered the forts at Vellore and Jinji in Madras.

His center of power and growth became the fort of Raigad. In fact, Raigad became Shivaji's capital city. Perched on top of a hill that was split off from the Western Ghats, the fort was virtually inaccessible from three sides. It is said that prizes were given to those who tried innovative methods to reach the top.

Raigad was filled with splendid monuments and massive gates and was an architectural wonder. Shivaji ruled from the glorious Raigad fort for six years. It was a time of great prosperity and justice. He had the best interests of his people in mind. The farmers loved him. When they complained to Shivaji about the unjust zamindari system, he took away the lands of the zamindars and distributed them among the peasants.

The monument built in memory of Shivaji at Raigad.

Efforts were made to teach Sanskrit to the people.

Under his rule, the 'untouchables' (the lowest caste) were given true justice. They were recruited in the army and also promoted.

He also laid great emphasis on education. He ensured that the Sanskrit language was not lost. He had Persian words replaced with Sanskrit ones wherever possible.

Religion too, was given due importance. He encouraged the people who had been converted to Islam under Aurangzeb and were unhappy, to reconvert to their old faith. He ensured that due respect is given to Mosques, Muslim places of worship and also to Muslim women. As a result, a large number of Muslims served in his army.

Because of these qualities, Shivaji was able to instill the same passion for revolution against the Mughals in the minds of his people. He inspired the people

Sambhaji

Shahu

so much that the Maratha Empire continued to fight the Mughal rule for 27 years after his death, despite the lack of proper leadership.

In 1680, he breathed his last. He was succeeded by his son, Raje Sambhaji who was later captured, tortured and killed by Aurangzeb.

Soon, there was no central authority among the Marathas, but there were individual commanders or Sardars who fought individual battles against the Mughals.

For over twenty years, Aurangzeb tried to quell the Maratha powers. After he died, the Marathas reunited under the leadership of Shahu, Shivaji's grandson. Shahu ruled as Emperor till 1749.

Shahu appointed a Peshwa or Prime Minister as head of government. After Shahu

The Marathas waged fierce battles against the British.

died, the Peshwas became the leaders of the Empire while Shivaji's descendents remained nominal rulers from Satara. During the 18th century, the Marathas managed to keep the British out of India. But soon after, the Peshwas and Sardars had conflicting interests and their peace fell apart.

After the Third Battle of Panipat in 1761, the Peshwas lost control of their Kingdom. Thereafter, many Sardars became Kings of their regions. When the British entered India, most of the former Maratha Empire was merged into their own Empire. The Marathas waged three fierce battles against the British. The result was that the British annexed the territory that had been ruled by the Peshwas. Thus, ended a great Empire that had ruled major parts of Central and Southern India efficiently.

Chapter - 25

The Kingdom of Mysore

Hyder Ali

Mysore palace

One of the prominent Southern dynasties, the Wodeyar Dynasty ruled the Kingdom of Mysore. The Kings, Hyder Ali and his son, Tipu Sultan made their mark in this region.

Born at Budikote around 1720 in Mysore (present-day Karnataka), Hyder Ali started his career as a soldier. He was a petty officer in the army, assistant to the Nizam, who was the Mughal deputy in South India. When the Nizam was assassinated, a lot of confusion followed. In the midst of the chaos, Hyder Ali's services attracted the attention of Nanjaraja, the minister of the Raja of Mysore. Hyder now received an independent command and over the next 12 years the minister and the King came to depend on him and were under his control.

But Mysore went bankrupt under Nanjaraja, and Hyder Ali slowly rose in ranks until he replaced the King.

He now extended his lands to the North beyond the Tungabhadra River. Hyder Ali spent much of his time building up a strong army to deal with two enemies; the Marathas in the Northwest and the British on the East and West coast.

After four damaging wars that the Marathas waged against him, their leader, Peshwa Madhavrao I died in 1772. Hyder Ali now pressed his advantage and extended his territory up to the river Krishna.

In the meantime, Hyder Ali had sought the friendship of the British in order to defeat the Marathas, but they wanted to undermine his power and use him. This resulted in the First Anglo-Mysore War in 1767. Hyder Ali's strong army forced the British to sign a mutual defense treaty with him. But when the Marathas attacked, the British went back on their word.

First Anglo Mysore War

Tipu Sultan   *Tipu was an avid reader.*

In 1780, Hyder Ali waged his second war against the British. He was defending his Kingdom as best as he could, when he suddenly died of cancer.

Succeeding him was his son Tipu Sultan, whom he had educated and trained well. Tipu ended up learning many languages, mathematics and science. He had a tremendous appetite for learning. He was also an avid reader and filled his library with more than 2000 books in different languages.

At a very young age, Tipu was given a wide exposure to both military and political affairs. When he was 15, his father began taking him on all his military campaigns. In fact, he headed the army in the First Anglo-Mysore War and defeated Colonel Braithwaite on the banks of the Coleroon.

In 1772, Tipu was sent to Northern Mysore to recover territories seized by the

The British suffered a humiliating defeat.

Marathas. He gained valuable experience in both warfare and diplomacy there.

During the Second Anglo-Mysore War in 1780, Tipu Sultan intercepted the British troops under Colonel Baillie as they moved South. He stopped them before they joined Sir Hector Munro in Kanchipuram.

With a massive army, Tipu completely subdued the Colonel and his men. Even when Munro sent reinforcements, they were no match for Tipu's troops. The British suffered a humiliating defeat. Munro fled to save his life. Colonel Baillie was arrested, however, and put in prison.

Chapter - 26

The Reign of Tipu Sultan

Tipu's alliance with the French

After his father's death, Tipu took over the throne and proved to be an able ruler. His first goal was to curb the advances of the British, who had set up the East India Company ostensibly for trading, but were trying to establish their supremacy in India. To this end, he tried to form alliances with the Marathas and the Mughals. But his suggestions for pacts and treaties were rejected. He now turned to another avenue, the French. They agreed and the Treaty of Versailles was signed. Tipu also formed an alliance with the Amir of Afghanistan and the Sultan of Turkey.

By now, the British were scared of Tipu's power. They signed a treaty with the Nizam of Hyderabad and the Marathas, who had rejected Tipu's entreaty.

In 1789, Tipu attacked the British colony at Travancore and triggered off the Third

Anglo-Mysore War. The battle lasted three years and was unfortunate for Tipu. The French backed out of their treaty at the last moment due to the French Revolution taking place in their homeland.

Thus, Tipu was defeated. Tipu was forced to give up half his Kingdom and pay a fine of 33 million rupees to the British! Even his two sons were taken hostage by Lord Cornwallis in lieu of the fine.

But, Tipu quietly started to rebuild his army. He paid off the fine and got his sons back. He slowly ragained his power as well.

His constant resistance to the British power earned him the nickname of the Tiger of Mysore. He adopted the Tiger as his official symbol. All his personal belongings were decorated with motifs of the animal or its stripes. In fact, his soldiers too, wore a tiger jacket and painted stripes on themselves.

Tipu's symbol - The Tiger.   *A soldier's Helmet, Shield and Sword.*

Tipu wrote the 'Futuh-ul-Majahdin' and 'Farmen ba Nam Ali Raja'.

Although most of his time as a King was spent in preparing for war, he ensured that his rule was just and secure. He built roads, tanks and dams. He also introduced several new industries and promoted trade and commerce.

His new and innovative methods included the introduction of sericulture, breeding finer varieties of ox, application of European military technology and adopting the politics of secularism.

Tipu had not lost his passion for learning. He had an impressive collection of literature right from Sanskrit works, tenth-century translations of the Quran, manuscripts of Mughal victories and several more.

In fact, Tipu wrote the 'Futuh-ul-Majahdin' and 'Farmen ba Nam Ali Raja', both published as a collection of letters.

He also built a large number of forts and palaces, most of which were demolished by the British after his death.

One of his most famous creations is the Daria Daulat, his summer palace at Srirangapatnam, his capital city. The name means 'wealth of the sea' and this beautiful palace was built in 1784.

In 1799, the new governor, General Richard Wellesley, was on a mission to destroy Tipu Sultan. Within two months, three armies marched towards Mysore. One was headed by the British Commander-in-Chief, the other two being the armies from Bombay and Madras. They soon reached Srirangapatnam. Thus, began the Fourth Anglo-Mysore War.

Tipu was unprepared for the fierce attack by the British. Though Tipu's fort was

Daria Daulat - Tipu's summer palace at Srirangapatnam

Tipu Sultan's Tomb

said to be nearly impenetrable, the British, nevertheless broke through the walls and surrounded the palace.

A furious battle ensued, with Tipu fighting like a tiger. When all hope was lost, he raced back to the palace to kill the royal women folk, for he knew they would rather die than fall into the hands of the British. But before he could reach them, he was shot and killed at the entrance gateway itself.

He was buried at a mausoleum that he had built himself. He was the most powerful of all native Princes of India and the biggest threat to the British position in Southern India.

Chapter - 27

BRITISH INDIA
The East India Company

The East India Company building at Calcutta (now Kolkata)

With the arrival of the Portugese explorer, Vasco da Gama, in 1498 at Calicut in South India, European explorers started landing on Indian shores. Their prime purpose was the profitable spice trade.

At the end of 1600, Queen Elizabeth of England allowed a large body of merchants to form a new trading company to trade with East Indies, India and Southeast Asia, which was later known as The East India Company. Over the next decade the merchants made twelve voyages to India. In 1617, Sir Thomas Roe approached the Mughal Emperor, Jahangir and sought his permission to build a factory in Surat. In two years, the permission was granted.

When the British started trading in the subcontinent, no one had dreamed that it could ever amount to more than peaceful trading. As Mughal power declined, the British influence increased. The reason was that Indian rulers were not well-disciplined while facing the British army and were no match for them.

Within ten years, another factory opened at Bombay, which became the headquarters of the company. Soon, the region was divided into three Presidencies; Calcutta, Bombay and Madras. Each presidency functioned by itself, but was responsible to the Court of Directors in London. The Company cleverly followed a triangular trade. They exchanged English gold and silver coins for Indian goods. Then they utilised these in China to subsidize the prices of commodities they bought there. With this system the Company earned huge profits and become richer.

India had been involved in world trade for centuries but it had never before

Within ten years another factory opened at Bombay.

Peasant landowners were forced to pay tax.

experienced the kind of exploitation that the British subjected it to. Under The East India Company, a large number of small Indian states were forced to pay subsidies for military protection against neighbouring enemies. The only states that remained independent were those that became allies of the British and paid a tribute to them.

The Company was corrupt and it drained their profits. This increased the need to collect higher revenues. Peasant landowners were forced to pay their taxes in cash. They in turn approached moneylenders, who seized their lands on their failure to repay the loans. There was widespread discontent and anger.

In 1757, a military force led by Robert Clive defeated the army of the Nawab of Bengal, Siraj-ud-daulah. With this victory, The East India Company was transformed from an association of traders into rulers of a large, unknown land.

Practice of 'Sati' was banned.

From this moment was born the British Raj.

By 1765, the Company had taken over Bengal. They also exercised the right to collect revenues on behalf of the Mughal Emperor in Bihar and Orissa.

Warren Hastings, the Governor General of Bengal, consolidated the military victories and established the fact that they were not answerable to the Mughals.

The British justified their rule by claims that there was a need for Indians to be 'civilized'. They sought to replace Indian systems with a more reliable method of justice, law and fair play. There were some religious practices that the British banned, like 'Sati'.

Over the next few decades, under the governor-generals, Dalhousie and Canning, the British took over even more territories. Their excuse was that the

British Invasion of the Sikh empire

rulers of these territories were corrupt or incapable or that they had no descendents. Smaller Kingdoms like Sambalpur, Baghat, Jhansi, Nagpur and Awadh fell into this trap.

The British could not take over Punjab, as the Sikhs were a dominant force under King Ranjit Singh. Punjab was safe from British invasion until his death. After that the British forces started to move in, causing the end of the Sikh Empire. In 1839, the British seized Sindh, Karachi, Sukkur and Bukkur (all in present-day Pakistan).

Chapter - 28

The Sepoy Mutiny

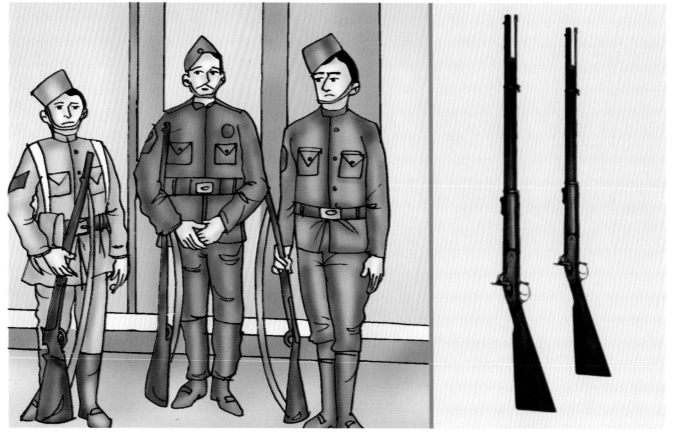

Gurkha Soldiers   Enfield rifles

During the British Raj, unrest and discontent spread all over India. Soon, many rebellions occurred in different parts of the country. The causes for these were many. The Hindu soldiers protested against the addition of Gurkha, Sikh and lower caste soldiers to their ranks. Moreover, the economic policies of the British Raj had an adverse effect on the soldiers' families back home, particularly in the Bengal presidency where soldiers came from Uttar Pradesh, Bihar and West Bengal, and this caused further unrest among the Sepoy troops.

The last straw was the use of animal grease on cartridges of the newly introduced Enfield rifles. To load the rifles the soldiers had to bite off the end of the cartridges. There was either pig or cow fat in the grease, which violated the religious code of the Muslim and Hindu soldiers.

In 1857, three regiments of soldiers refused to use the ammunition for the Enfield rifles. They were disbanded. Then, 85 soldiers disobeyed orders to load their rifles. They were arrested. The remaining soldiers mutinied on May 19, 1857. They then marched to Delhi and demanded that the last Mughal Emperor, Bahadur Shah Zafar, take over as the ruler of India and the head of the rebels. Though he reluctantly agreed, the British defeated and later exiled him to Burma where he died in 1862.

This uprising came to be known as the Sepoy Mutiny or the Revolt of 1857. One famous soldier at Barrackpore, Mangal Pandey, attacked his British sergeant. He was arrested and hanged the following month.

Soon, another regiment revolted. Ninety thousand of the Bengal Army's Sepoy force had joined the mutiny. Initially the British were unable to respond to the uprising and suffered heavy casualties. After extensive losses at Kanpur and

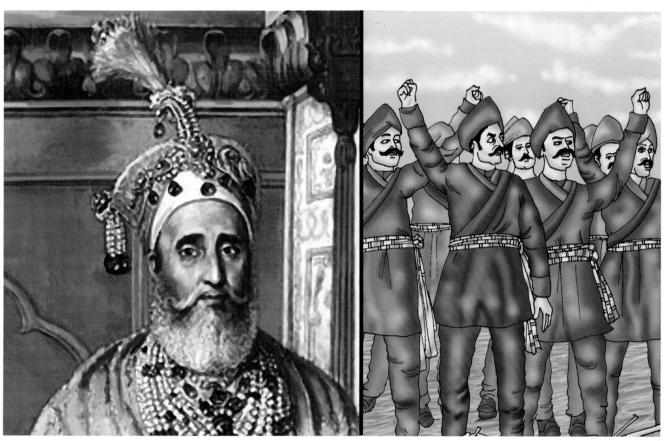

Bahadur Shah Zafar   *Soldiers disobeyed orders to load the rifles.*

145

British Parliament in England.

Lucknow, the British Army sought the help of loyal Sikh and Gurkha forces. As the revolt spread throughout India, the British fought the main army of rebels near Delhi and drove them back, effectively suppressing the rebellion.

In response to the Mutiny, the British Parliament passed an act that abolished The East India Company. India became a Crown Colony to be governed by the British Parliament directly. A British cabinet member, the Secretary of State for India, and the Governor General looked after Indian affairs.

In the following year, Queen Victoria conferred the title of Viceroy on the Governor-General of India. Her policy was 'Divide and Rule' to prevent the Indians from uniting to rebel against her rule. In this way, the British sought accommodations with Princes and landlords, in turn allowing them a degree of freedom. This ensured their loyalty. The army was reorganized to avoid further conspiracies.

An Indian Railway Station

Now the British turned their attention to commerce and development. The first step was the building of a transport system to move imported British readymade goods and to export Indian raw materials. Construction of the railroad and railway stations began and many new towns came into existence just to transport Indian resources to the markets. New roads were built, a new communications system came into existence and a harbour was built in Bombay.

However, the conditions of the poor deteriorated. Village artisans went broke as a result of competition from English machine-made goods. The destruction of the Indian craft industry forced many into poverty and they had to turn to tilling land for a living.

During the American Civil War, Indian agriculture shifted from foodstuffs to cotton for supply to the English textile industry. This and a severe drought in the 1870s led to a terrible famine that spread throughout India.

Chapter - 29

The Indian Nationalist Movement

The British tried to integrate high-caste Indians into the government.

The British now started a program of reform. They tried to integrate high-caste Indians and rulers into the government. They stopped confiscating lands, advocated religious tolerance and allowed Indians into civil service in subordinate roles. They increased the number of British soldiers and only they were allowed to handle artillery. In 1877, Queen Victoria took the title of 'Empress of India'.

The British sought to 'civilise' the Indians through conversion to Christianity. But these efforts failed. The other alternative was education. A system of westernized education was introduced and a new educated class of Indians emerged. They were the mediators between the British and the rest of Indian society. This class found its way into the government as lawyers, businessmen, journalists and teachers.

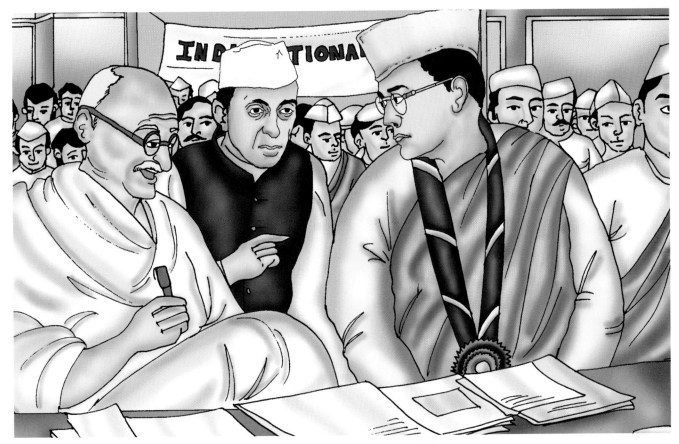

Meeting of the Indian National Congress

Hinduism survived despite the best efforts of the British to advocate conversion to Christianity and in fact, achieved a revival. In addition, Indians, who had been trained to believe in western ideals of justice and freedom, started to protest against the discrimination by the British.

Thus was born the Indian National Congress in 1885. It was created to address the charges against British officials who prevented Indians from assuming control over their own affairs. Eventually, the Congress became the driving force behind Indian nationalism and the freedom struggle .

Initial efforts against the British were not well organised. This led to the rise of a rebel group who were extremists and gave Indian nationalism a distinctly Hindu orientation, which alienated the Muslims.

This resulted in the formation of the All India Muslim League in 1906. The League forcefully promoted loyalty to the British and the advancement of Muslim political interests.

But some Muslims began to feel isolated, especially as the British promoted Christianity. More Muslims started to join the Congress party. By 1916, the Muslim League and the Congress signed the Lucknow Pact. They were now united in their cause to drive out the British. An important member of the Congress was Muhammad Ali Jinnah who worked towards a separate State for the Muslims, Pakistan. Eventually this caused a major strife between the two religious groups and led to much violence and bloodshed later on.

Soon, there was a rise in the number of radicals like the group led by Bal Gangadhar Tilak, who believed that Swaraj was every Indian's birthright. Tilak wanted to assault the British directly.

Muhammad Ali Jinnah

The Partition of Bengal

Dhaka

The Swadeshi movement had many Indians protesting against the use of British goods.

Other Bengal rebels carried out a campaign of terror and assassination against the British. In 1905, the British partitioned Bengal and this led to the first major resistance to foreign rule.

The Swadeshi movement was born, and the Indians protested in various ways - boycott of foreign goods, strikes, non-cooperation, non-violent resistance, etc. Finally, the British revoked the partition. Their motive had been to divide the Hindus who dominated West Bengal, and the Muslims who were a majority in East Bengal.

The Freedom Struggle

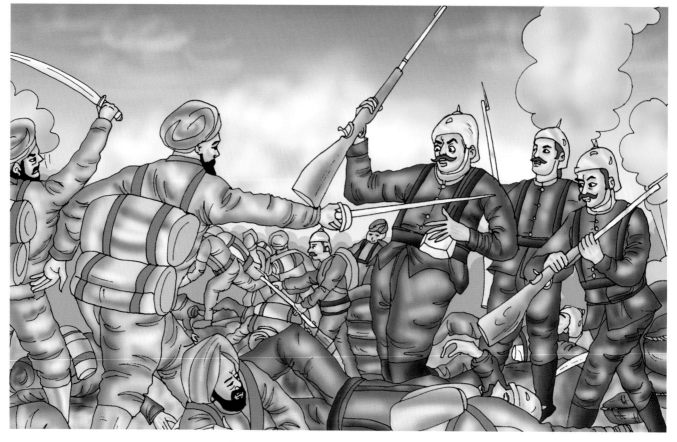

Indian Soldiers in World War I.

The Independence struggle began in earnest.

There were several influential men like Swami Vivekananda, Ramakrishna Paramahamsa, Aurobindo, Subramanya Bharati, Tagore and others, who spread the passion for freedom among the Indians.

During World War I Britain declared that India was also at war with Germany along with England. A large number of Indian troops served abroad. When the war concluded, the British imposed stricter legislation in India to curb those people they felt were political extremists.

To cover war expenses, Indians were heavily taxed and trade was disrupted.

Indian soldiers started smuggling arms into India to overthrow the British rule.

In the midst of this emerged the man the country began to revere, Mohandas Karamchand Gandhi. He became the undisputed leader of the Nationalist Movement.

Gandhi had been a leader of the anti-apartheid movement in South Africa. He advocated the policy of Satyagraha and of non-violent civil disobedience. The latter meant that Indians would have to stop cooperating with the British Government. Mahatma Gandhi, as he came to be known, had the unique ability to inspire millions of common people. His vision took the freedom struggle to the national level.

In 1919, the Rowlatt Act was passed and it came to be known as the Black Act.

Mahatma Gandhi had a great vision for the people of India.

The Jallianwala Bagh tragedy

The Act gave the Government the right to silence the press, arrest political activists or anyone they considered suspicious and keep them in prison without a trial.

In April 1919, there was a terrible massacre at the Jallianwala Bagh in Amritsar. General Dyer gave the order to kill hundreds of unarmed civilians, including women and children, who were attending a meeting at the Bagh that was closed from three sides. This action triggered off nation-wide hatred for the British rule.

The Non-Cooperation Movement was launched. Gandhi called for the boycott of British educational institutions and courts. The movement urged people to refuse to pay taxes and forsake British titles or honours. This posed a serious problem to the governing body.

In 1920, a new and reorganised Congress was formed with Swaraj as their only

The Dandi March

goal. Prominent leaders like Jawaharlal Nehru, Subhash Chandra Bose and Vallabhai Patel emerged.

The Indian leaders now called for complete independence from Britain and threatened nation-wide civil disobedience. Gandhi embarked on the 'Salt Satyagraha' or the 'Dandi March', a march of about 400 kilometres from Ahmedabad to Dandi. This was to protest against British taxes on salt, and at Dandi, they broke the law by making their own salt from seawater.

The British responded to the civil disobedience through widespread arrests and firing on crowds. Gandhi too, went to jail many times.

The Congress and the Government remained in conflict over the next few years. In 1935, the Government of India Act was passed, a last effort to restore British India. The Act allowed an election and the Congress emerged as the dominant

Bhagat Singh   *Chandrashekhar Azad*

party. During this time the rift between them and the Muslim League continued to grow.

Jinnah, the President of the Muslim League, insisted that a separate Muslim state, called Pakistan, be carved out of British India to safeguard the interest of the Muslim community.

In the meantime, the armed rebellion against the British started to grow and several rebel groups arose in many parts of India. Several murders occurred and looting began, with many revolutionaries being captured and imprisoned. Leaders like Chandrasekhar Azad, Bhagat Singh and Batukeshwar Dutt led acts of violence against the British. But soon the revolutionary activities died down and many rebels joined political parties.

Chapter - 31

Quit India

The Quit India Movement

In 1942, Gandhi launched the Quit India Movement, which demanded the immediate independence from Britain and protested against sending Indians to fight in World War II.

Talks between the Congress and the British failed and the former endorsed the Quit India Movement. Indians were urged to act as an independent nation and not follow the orders of the British.

Gandhi and other important Congress leaders were imprisoned. Large-scale protests broke out all over the country. Strikes were called which were followed by bomb attacks, sabotage and violence. The Muslim League declared its support for the British side and therefore had the freedom to spread the message of Islam.

British planes dropped bombs.

In the meantime, the British responded to the protests through mass arrests, fines and airdropping of bombs. The rebel movement which had resorted to violence to gain independence was actually working against Gandhi's principles of non-violence. This resulted in the movement being leaderless and petered out over the next year.

In 1946, the Royal Indian Navy called a strike and Indian sailors too, mutinied. The strike spread and the Indian population supported it. Soon, the Air Force and the local police forces joined in. There were more riots and revolts.

Chapter -32

Independence

Lord Mountbatten   *Clement Atlee*

Finally, the British Prime Minister, Clement Atlee declared that India would be granted independence. Now negotiations started among the major political parties and communities, especially the Sikhs, the Congress and the Muslim League.

In 1946, the Muslim League launched Direct Action Day. The purpose was to convey that an undivided India was no longer possible.

On June 3rd, 1947, Viscount Louis Mountbatten, the last British Governor General of India announced the partitioning of India into a secular India and a Muslim Pakistan.

On 14th August, Pakistan was declared a separate nation with Muhammad Ali Jinnah as the new Governor General.

At midnight on 15th August, 1947, India was declared Independent.

Although a joyous occasion, there were violent clashes between Hindus, Muslims and Sikhs. The partition did not come without its horrors. At least 500,000 people were said to have been killed and many women were abducted. About 11 million Hindus, Muslims and Sikhs crossed borders, the Muslims from India to Pakistan and the Hindus and Sikhs into the new, divided India from Pakistan.

In the midst of all this confusion, Prime Minister Nehru urged Mountbatten to continue as Governor General until the next year, when he was replaced by Rajagopalachari.

India was declared Independent.

Mahatma Gandhi's Samadhi at Rajghat, New Delhi

In 1948 Gandhi was assasinated and the nation mourned for him. In another two years, the constitution was drafted, and on 26th Jaunary, 1950, the Republic of India was proclaimed. Dr. Rajendra Prasad became the first President of India, taking over from Rajagopalachari.

After decades of conflict India finally tasted freedom. Despite being free of British rule, India still retains some of their influence, especially in the educational system, the use of the English language, the printing press, cricket, etc.

Ever since our country came into being, it has been a mix of diverse cultures and societies. India's history has always been rich and interesting, producing some of the greatest leaders the world has ever seen. In the last half century, India has experienced rapid and progressive development that has brought it much prominence in the world stage.

Republic Day Parade on January 26.

Many predicted that India, because of its cultural diversity, would break up into smaller countries. However, with all its problems, India has survived as a sovereign country with a democratic identity and its cultural diversity as its uniqueness. The Constitution of India, drafted by Dr. B. R. Ambedkar, was adopted when India became a Republic on January 26, 1950.

Even after independence, Goa remained under Portuguese rule. However, on December 19, 1961, it was annexed to India when the Indian Army, backed by the Air Force, ended the Portuguese rule. India had its first war with China in 1962 which ended in India's defeat, as India was not prepared for such wars. However, India had a second war with Pakistan in 1965 that it won decisively. During a subsequent Indo-Pak War in 1971, that India again won, Bangladesh was created out of East Pakistan. The Five-Year plans initiated since 1951, have brought about all-round development. Despite a huge population, the Green Revolution started

Chandrayaan-I space mission that concluded in May 2009.

in 1965, has made India self-sufficient in food-grains production. Now India is also the largest producer of milk and milk products.

On May 18, 1974, India conducted its first ever nuclear test at Pokharan in Rajasthan. Since then many scientific milestones have been achieved, The latest one is the Chandrayaan-I space mission that concluded in May 2009 where possible water spots were identified on the Moon. With the boom in Information Technology (IT), India has become an IT hub and large foreign corporations have set up base in India. Despite growth and progress, there were some dark chapters in the post-independence period. The assassination of Prime Minister, Indira Gandhi, in 1984 and of Prime Minister, Rajiv Gandhi in 1991, as well as the demolition of the Babri Mosque in Ayodhya in 1992 were major setbacks. In 1999, during the Kargil Conflict, the Pakistan Army and ISI backed militants (Mujahideens), seized many strategic locations inside the Indian territory in

Modern mall in North India.

Kashmir. However, India recaptured all the areas forcing the Mujahideens to retreat. India has produced world-class scientists, doctors, engineers, journalists, sportspersons and bureaucrats. Today, India, against all odds with over a billion people, stands as the largest democracy in the world. Improved relations with many countries particularly the United States and the European Union, and a dynamic, fast growing economy that is predicted to take over the United States of America by 2050, India is now being looked at as a potential superpower.

Today, modern India is catching up with the Western world with tall buildings and huge malls visible in many of its big cities. India is just below China and USA as regards mobile phone users. Bollywood, India's film industry, producing almost 1,000 films a year, has already surpassed Hollywood. India is poised to become one of the most fascinating and most visited countries of the world.